A Winner's Faith

Takieya J. Jones

Trilogy Christian Publishers
A Wholly Owned Subsidiary of Trinity Broadcasting Network
2442 Michelle Drive
Tustin, CA 92780
Copyright © 2021 by Takieya Jones

All Scripture quotations, unless otherwise noted, taken from
THE HOLY BIBLE, NEW INTERNATIONAL VERSION®,
NIV® Copyright © 1973, 1978, 1984, 2011 by Biblica, Inc.®
Used by permission. All rights reserved worldwide.
Scripture quotations marked (KJV) taken from The Holy Bible,
King James Version. Cambridge Edition: 1769.

For information, address Trilogy Christian Publishing
Rights Department, 2442 Michelle Drive, Tustin, Ca 92780.
Trilogy Christian Publishing/ TBN and colophon are trademarks
of Trinity Broadcasting Network.
For information about special discounts for bulk purchases,
please contact Trilogy Christian Publishing.
Manufactured in the United States of America

10 9 8 7 6 5 4 3 2 1
Library of Congress Cataloging-in-Publication Data is available.
ISBN 978-1-64773-965-2
ISBN 978-1-64773-966-9 (ebook)

DEDICATION

This book is dedicated to the One Who is Faithful and True,
the Giver of all Life, and the Lover of my soul—King Jesus.
May you be glorified in this body of work.

ACKNOWLEDGMENTS

To my family, friends, and the "House of Love," thank you for your support and encouragement over the years. You all are wonderful blessings in my life.

To my mother, Susie, thank you for teaching me the Lord's Prayer, for giving me my first *The Rainbow Study Bible®*, and for being my earliest example of what it means to walk by faith. To my father, Brutus, thank you for always showing up for me and for displaying strength in adversity. You will forever be in my heart.

Special thanks to World Changers Bible School (Gathering of Messengers™ facilitator Dr. Robyn L. Norwood) for having the vision and providing the resources to equip and prepare God's people to become the authors they desire to be.

TABLE OF CONTENTS

FOREWORD

It is quite amazing to know that there is a worthy comparison between the human heart and the spiritual heart. There is anatomy about both that will aid the believer in navigating the life of faith. In *A Winner's Faith*, author Takieya J. Jones explains to the reader exactly what that comparison is and how vital it is to become familiar with it so that we can self-assess when preparing the soil of our hearts to receive from God.

In this book, Takieya has chosen to teach and lead through transparency. If you are an influencer of any kind—whether you are a parent, educational leader, spiritual leader, social symbol, or the like—you may understand that honesty and boldness are of great value when the aim is to ensure that people gain value and direction after reading, viewing, or hearing your material. In a unique and inspiring fashion, Takieya has chosen to do just that by sharing her own real-life stories, illustrations, and experiences that make the message within this book hit home. Her approach is relevant and effective, prompting her reader to take immediate action and make the necessary adjustments in their belief system to begin to walk by faith truly.

Her message will turn your thoughts and attention toward the factors that are taken into account when we have set our hearts on trusting God and the process that leads to the kind of success that only He can give. Takieya shows other believers and even non-believers alike how faith really works; that is God's kind of faith. She does this in a number of ways. First, by sharing the importance of hope in the believer's heart. Hope is the reason why many of us have chosen to believe in the first place, and it plays a vital role where faith is concerned.

She also presents food for thought for the reader to ponder, such as how the Bible defines faith, whether or not we can believe God for the things we deeply desire in this life, what it means to have a hardened heart, and what to do when our surroundings and environment are presenting a complete contradiction to what we believe God for and what we are positioning ourselves to receive.

Takieya also goes deep into the fabric of faith, which is love. She shines light on the fact that faith can not work without the presence of love (Galatians 5:6). Her declaration to her readers is that Jesus is love and the love which was expressed in the sacrifice of the person of Jesus Christ, by default, makes us winners.

Without a doubt, every reader of this book will experience significant change when they allow the Gospel within this message to come into their hearts and live. Hope, love, and understanding are all change agents, and Takieya has availed herself to the task and the labor of producing a phenomenal title that will ignite transformation.

Dr. Robyn L. Norwood

Norwood Literary Enterprises, LLC

PREFACE

There is something to be said about a believer that can't be stopped. When faced with what seems like insurmountable circumstances, they refuse to cave in and quit. They have the ability to go through the fire and come out without the smell of smoke. What I'm describing is the faith of a winner!

The faith of a winner does not waiver or crumble under pressure. There will come a time in every person's life where they will be faced with a trial that seems impossible in the natural. You may look at the facts concerning the situation, and it may seem completely hopeless. But when you have made a quality decision to stand on the promises of God, no matter what, you will never lose. Don't settle for second best. When you have done all to stand, keep on standing. God will honor His Word.

The idea and vision stemmed from my personal testimony of being a contest winner, which resulted in me leaving a car lot with a brand-new debt-free vehicle! This is the story of an ordinary girl with a typical day-to-day life who decided to step out on faith that yielded extraordinary results. In this book, *A*

Winner's Faith, I share how I have applied the Word of God to a practical need and how it yielded tangible results.

God wants to be our Father. He doesn't want us to struggle with anything in life, and He cares about the smallest things we think may be insignificant. In this book, God has instructed me to share the very basics of what I've learned about faith, how people in the Bible used faith to overcome life challenges, and how He desires for people in this generation to learn how to trust and rely on Him for everything. I will use a fair amount of Scripture references, as this is the basis and foundation for what I believe to be a winner's faith. And because I believe words are very important, I will also be exploring the origin of various words, as they have been translated from the original Greek, Hebrew, or Aramaic languages.

My heart is to share with readers what I have personally found to be the truth of the gospel as it has been revealed to me by the Holy Spirit as I continue to walk with and seek the Lord. I do find it helpful when studying the Word of God to study the Scriptures with study guides and resources (like Bible concordances) that are available.

The ultimate goal of faith is to bring you to a place of having an unshakable reliance upon God, who is Love. In this love relationship, God wants you to receive total salvation, which means a life of abundance in not just some areas but every area of life. You need to reach the place of knowing that in Christ Jesus, nothing is impossible for you. God wants you to use your faith to believe Him for a prosperous life here on earth, as it already is in heaven.

If you are open to learning, God will meet you where you are. Anyone who hungers and thirsts after righteousness shall be fulfilled. If you want practical tips on how to stand on the promises of God to see proven results in your life, keep reading!

―――――――

"Today, I have given you the choice between life and death, between blessings and curses. Now I call on heaven and earth to witness the choice you make. Oh, that you would choose life so that you and your descendants might live!"

Deuteronomy 30:19 (NLT)

―――――――

INTRODUCTION

Faith to Choose Life

A re you ready to start using your faith to win in life? Imagine two boxes sitting in front of you. Box number one is labeled "life," and box number two is labeled "death." Inside box number one is "The Blessing," and inside box number two is "The Curse." You have been given the option to choose either box. Unlike *Let's Make a Deal* or some similar television game show, the contents of these boxes have been uncovered for you.

The chief executive officer (CEO) knows that life is a series of decisions. To help you out, he has laid all the cards out in each box, so you can have the opportunity to make a wise choice. However, it does require you to examine both boxes thoroughly and take heed to what's written within each box to make the best choice. One box may appear more glamorous than the other, but you have been given specific instruction not to allow False Evidence Appearing Real to sway your decision.

The contents of box number two may seem as though they are more pleasurable, but box number one has an authentic truth within that tells you otherwise; however, it is ultimately your choice. Armed with this information, what are you going to do?

Your turn is up, and you are now faced with the decision to choose a box. The decision you are faced with may seem simple enough to make, but you begin to wonder, "Is this some sort of trick?" Is it as simple as just choosing a box, presumably the box labeled "life," as the CEO has laid out in box number one?

When it comes to real life, the Bible tells us we do have a choice. We can either choose life (God's Life and all The Blessing that comes with it) or Satan's death (and all the curse that comes with it). We are constantly facing decisions we must make in life, some big and some small. And you may not realize it, but the decisions we are faced with lend themselves to lean one way or the other. There is no grey area.

We also often find ourselves facing the decision of how to respond in situations that we find ourselves in. Particularly those situations that are challenging and apply some sort of pressure on us. This pressure is often on our minds, and it is designed to make you quit; or, as in the example of the boxes, the pressure that causes you to choose box number two, maybe without even considering or fully comprehending the consequences you may face in choosing the wrong box.

When you are faced with a challenging situation in life, the first step you must take to win over the situation and not be overcome by it is to make a quality decision to choose life. When I say, "choose life," I specifically mean you must make a conscious heartfelt decision to choose to believe what the Word of God has to say about the situation or the problem you are facing.

If you have a need in life, choose to believe that God has already made provision for that need, and it requires faith in God to believe for that need to be met. God's Word is Life. Jesus said in John 6:63 (KJV), "...the words that I speak unto you, they are spirit, and they are life." You must choose to believe what the Word of God has to say over what you may see, over what you feel, and other voices that may be communicating something different. Ask yourself, "What does the Word have to say about this?" No matter how bad or bleak it may look, choosing the "life" box, by default, will mean you are choosing to believe God—no matter what.

As you go forward reading this book, remember the scenario of the two boxes. I will refer to this a few more times throughout. One example of how God used His Word to prove Himself to me was through my experience of becoming an actual contest winner. But this can be paralleled to any facet of life. In the Spirit realm, if you are a born-again believer, you are a winner! What is on the inside will begin to move on the outside and affect your physical life.

Someone may be asking, "If I'm not born-again, does that

mean I'm a loser?" I will put it this way: If you are not a born-again believer in Jesus, that means Satan continues to have authority over your life. Power and authority over the entire earth and everything in it was handed over to the devil at the beginning of time when the first man and woman (Adam and Eve) sinned in the Garden of Eden. Even though God gave specific instructions, they let an outside deceptive voice sway them into believing there was something more appealing that God was withholding from them.

So, no matter how hard you try to overcome Satan, you will eventually lose the battle, and he will win over you. Even worse, if you die without ever making Jesus the Lord of your life, that means you forfeit the blessing of heaven in exchange for an eternity in hell. You will forever be subjected to Satan's torment in eternal damnation. Hell was not made for people, only for the devil and fallen angels that rebelled against God. But the good news is, Jesus has conquered hell, death, and the grave! Jesus has taken the authority back, and Satan no longer has any place in the life of a person who makes Jesus their Lord.

The Bible clearly states that we have all sinned and come short of God's glory (Romans 3:23). The first step in having a winning faith is to recognize that without Jesus, you are a sinner who needs a Savior. You must have enough faith to take the first step in giving your heart to the Lord and allowing Him to be your guide in life. How does one get faith to take the first step? Good question! We will be exploring that more in section 1 of this book. But in this initial introduction, if you have never heard about the saving power of Jesus, faith is coming to you now as you hear the truth of who He is as you are reading these words.

Let the Words that Jesus spoke thousands of years ago become a living Word to you now. The Word of God will give you the faith to believe. Let Jesus prove to you that He is the all-knowing and all-powerful Savior of the world. Let Him prove to you that He is not a God of rules and laws but a God of Love, Mercy, and Grace. Be willing to forego any myths of what you've heard about religion and embrace the life of a genuine relationship with Jesus Christ.

If you are not a born-again believer in Jesus, I encourage you to give Him your life today! Whether you are saved or not, know that God will always love you. But God wants you to be saved because He wants to be your Father, your Lord, your faithful Friend forever. He does not want you to die, go to hell, and be lost for an eternity when He gave you eternal life through His Son Jesus.

You can run away from God for years, but when you stop running, He will still be there with open arms. If you are reading this book years or decades from when it was originally published, guess what? God is still here, and He is still waiting for you to receive Him. God is Love, and there is nothing you could ever do to get Him to stop loving you. God longs to be in fellowship with you, and it is very easy to receive from Him. It's as simple as saying, "Jesus, I believe in you."

21

When you believe in Jesus, you believe in the authority of the powerful Name of Jesus to save you. We can be confident in knowing this is true because Romans 10:9 says that if you confess with your mouth the Lord Jesus and believe in your heart that God raised Him from the dead, you will be saved. Faith to choose life is based on your confession of Jesus Christ as your Lord and Savior, giving Him your life, and receiving the gift of His precious Holy Spirit.

Another Bible passage that gives us faith to believe in Jesus's saving power is Acts 16:31 that says if you believe on the Lord Jesus Christ, you will be saved! It's as uncomplicated and wonderfully graceful as that. Jesus did the hard part. All we have to do is receive what He did for us. It is by grace through faith that we are saved. You don't have to work for your salvation; just believe.

Romans 10:10 goes on to say that with your heart, you believe unto righteousness, and with your mouth, your confession is made unto salvation. Your decision to choose life is a matter of the heart. Matters of the heart are very delicate and very important to how we experience this life. Both the physical heart and the heart of your Spirit will be discussed in a little more detail in section 2 of this book.

God tells us in His Word that every issue of life flows out of our hearts. The Bible also says that people look at your outward appearance and make assumptions about you, but God judges your heart. *You* have the authority over your own life to choose God's life over Satan's death.

Once you confess Jesus as your Lord and Savior, something supernatural happens in the spirit realm. You become a born-again believer in Jesus Christ, and God gives you a new nature, one of righteousness. This means you are in right standing with God because you chose to believe in His Son Jesus. You no longer have that old sin nature that led you down paths of destruction. God's Spirit moves within you. God says in Ezekiel 36:26 (NIV), "I will give you a new heart and put a new spirit in you."

If you've been longing for peace that you haven't been able to find in this world, there is an answer for you today. Call on the Name of the Lord, and He will save you. He will save you from whatever has been holding you captive. If you have made the confession of faith to receive Jesus today, let me be the first to welcome you into the family of God! You are now what the Bible calls a new creation in Christ Jesus. All of heaven rejoices when you make such a life-changing decision to give your life to the Lord. If you don't realize yet exactly what you've just done, let me tell you; You have just chosen box number one, the "life" box! You have just exercised your faith that came from hearing the truth of the Word of God and have chosen to live in eternal life!

Once you make a quality decision to confess Jesus as your Lord, you must repent and turn away from the ways of your sinful past and begin to seek after God's way of living. That's true repentance. It will take a renewal of your mind to know how to walk now a different way than you did before. To do this, you must find out from the Bible how God originally intended for you to live a prosperous and triumphant life before sin entered the world and brought destruction.

If you've never read the Word of God or are not consistent in reading, begin finding out about who God is and who He made you to be by spending time reading the Bible. Find a translation that you can understand so that you can read with comprehension. There is an undeniable joy that comes when you realize the freedom that comes when you make a quality decision to choose life. The truth of the Gospel of Jesus Christ is that He has made us winners in this life.

The Bible is the greatest book ever written in all of history. It is a book that chronicles a story of redemption and love after separation and death. At the end of God's story of time, it's love that wins. And if you are in Jesus Christ, you are engrafted into this love. If you never "win" anything in the material sense during your life, you can still rejoice today because you have already won in Christ Jesus in every way that matters. I offer to you that this is what having a winner's faith is all about.

You, dear reader, are about to embark on a wonderful journey of discovering faith. Along the way, I pray that you experience the added benefit of self-reflection, or maybe even a new discovery of who you are. More specifically, who you are in Christ Jesus. This book is divided into three main sections— Spirit, Soul, and Body, with three chapters in each section.

At the beginning of each section, a short prologue will introduce the upcoming chapters. At the end of each section, there will be an epilogue, which will be sure to inspire you to keep going on this personal faith journey until you reach the end. As you journey through each section, hear what the Spirit of God is speaking to you throughout. If you don't know how to hear God's voice, ask Him to help you develop your "inner ear" as you read this book. God is a Spirit, and He connects with you by way of your Spirit. Believe that you can hear God's voice because He desires to commune with you. And what God speaks to you will always line up with what He's already spoken in the Bible.

God inspired me to write this book, and I believe that He has something to say to you specifically. He already knows who you are, where you are in your life, and exactly what you need to hear in this season. If you are reading these words, that means this book is for you. The unearthing of faith and our continual discovery of the vastness of God can never really be exhausted or completed. As we grow and seek the Lord, we just go from one level of glory to the next. We will forever be in a state of learning more and more about the unfailing and never-ending love of God.

This book is just a snapshot in time of my revelations of faith, as it has been revealed and unfolded in my life up to this point. I hope there is something you take away that will be impactful to you in some way. So, hang on tight, for this is where we will begin an essential discussion on how the kingdom of God operates, dissect what true biblical faith is all about, and eventually find out how I used faith in God to believe and stand until the harvest of what I believed for showed up!

SECTION 1: SPIRIT
The Prologue

Welcome aboard! Congratulations on making the significant decision of learning more about how to have A Winner's Faith! The most important part of your faith journey will begin here with the Spirit. If you skipped the introduction section of this book, go back and read it! It provides a key foundation and a sort of "baptism" into this first part of your faith journey.

You are not just a body—you are a spirit being, you have a unique soul, and you live in a physical body. The real you... can't be seen with your physical eyes. The real you...God made just like Himself. In His very own image, God created_____ (insert your name). Wonderfully and beautifully made...That is who YOU are.

The very essence of who you are is just like God. "Really?" you may ask. Yes! Children often have some of the same mannerisms as their parents. So too, if you receive God as your Lord and Savior, He becomes your Father. As you spend time in His presence, fellowshipping and getting to know Him, you'll begin to act like Him and think as He thinks. But you must invite Him in if you want to win! Let us begin our journey!

———

"And when he was demanded of the Pharisees, when the kingdom of God should come, he answered them and said, 'The kingdom of God cometh not with observation: Neither shall they say, 'Lo here!' Or, 'lo there!' for behold, the Kingdom of God is within you.'"

Luke 17:20-21 (KJV)

———

CHAPTER 1

KINGDOM PRINCIPLES FOR KINGDOM RESULTS

In the Beginning, Was the Word

To have an understanding of how faith operates, you must first understand how the kingdom of God operates and how God created us to use faith to function on earth. If you are a person who is unfamiliar with scriptural principles, or if you aren't even aware that there is a spirit realm that is running concurrently to this physical, natural world, you may find it difficult to grasp how faith (a spiritual principle) is connected to manifestation (a physical outcome). To discover what it means to operate in faith as a born-again, spirit-filled believer, you must go back to the beginning of creation to see how God not only created the first man and woman by His Word but how He masterfully created the world as we know it.

You are not just what you see in the mirror. Look past what you see in the natural and see yourself as a spirit being. That's the real you, the eternal part of you that will live forever. As a spirit being, you and the spirit realm can only be perceived by what's revealed in God's Word. If you are born-again, who you are as a new creation in Christ Jesus must be received by faith according to what God's Word says about your new identity.

We know that God uniquely created the human as a three-part being (Spirit, soul, and body), which is revealed to the church in the book of 1 Thessalonians 5:23. Our Heavenly Father spoke mankind, both male and female (Genesis 1:26-27), into being before He even formed their physical bodies out of mere dust and breathed into them the breath of life. The formation of man's physical body was not spoken of until Genesis 2:7 (KJV), "And the Lord God formed man of the dust of the ground, and breathed into his nostrils the breath of life; and man became a living soul." In Genesis 2:21-22, the Bible then goes on to speak of how God took a rib from the first man (Adam) and made the first woman (Eve).

These passages reveal how God created us as a spirit being in His image and fashioned us after His likeness. Just as He did when creating the heaven and the earth and everything within, He created us by His Word—"And God said, Let us make man in our image..." (Genesis 1:26, KJV). Everything God did in creation, including the first humans that walked the earth, involved His Word. There were six days of creation in which God created the world. It is noted that He took the time to prepare a place (The garden of Eden) for His special creation so that they would have all they needed to dwell and prosper.

> *Life Application: You should know that when God calls you to a place, to a purpose in life, He prepares the place before He brings you there. Don't be afraid to step out when the Spirit of the Lord is leading you to move. Don't even worry about the provision. If God calls you to do it, the provision will be there as you step out in obedience and faith in what He told you to do.*

This very beginning of Bible history begins to reveal the power of faith, administered by the Holy Spirit through the spoken Word. It is important to know that God, who is a Spirit, by faith created things which are seen by things which do not appear (Hebrews 11:3, KJV). So the concept of words is not only important to the human experience in terms of how we communicate with one another, but God chose the spoken word as a mode of activating and creating.

As defined in our English terminology, a word is something that is said, talk, order, command, the act of speaking. Throughout Genesis, this is seen when God "said" the many things that He spoke into being. This is re-confirmed in Hebrews 11:3 (KJV) when it is revealed that "Through faith, we understand that the worlds were framed by the word of God..." The Greek word for "word" in this passage of Scripture is "Rhema," which is translated "an utterance; command[1]." The worlds were framed upon God's command. He said in Genesis

---

1   James Strong, 1995

1:3 (KJV), "…Let there be light: and there was light."

All You Need is Seed

In the book of Mark, chapter 4, Jesus compared the kingdom of God (God's system of operation) to a man planting a seed into the ground. In this parable that is about a sower, Jesus talks about the sower sowing the Word. Here in this text, "word" is translated from a different Greek word called "Logos." One translation of Logos can also be used to refer to "something said" (to include the overall communication process—the thought, also reasoning, or motive). But unlike Rhema, in the gospel of John, "Word" is translated as "the Divine Expression of Christ[2]." From other teachings I've come across, "Rhema" is most often used to refer to a spoken word, while Logos is referred to as the written word.

John 1:1-3 (KJV) says, "In the beginning was the Word, and the Word was with God, and the Word was God. The same was in the beginning with God. All things were made by him; and without him was not any thing made that was made." We know John is using "Word" to reference Jesus Christ because of verse 14, which reads, "And the Word was made flesh, and dwelt among us, (and we beheld his glory, the glory as of the only begotten of the Father,) full of grace and truth."

Jesus is the Word eloquently described in this text. When you connect these verses of Scripture in the book of John with the Scriptures describing creation in Genesis chapters 1 and

2   James Strong, 1995

2, it confirms that not only was God's spoken Word in the beginning, but Jesus the Word was in the beginning with God and was God. The same Word that became flesh in the miraculous birth of the Savior Jesus is the same Word that John reveals was at the beginning of time. The Father, the Son, and the Holy Spirit were all in the beginning as the Word of God was framing the worlds.

You cannot separate God from His Word. And you cannot separate His Word from its creative ability. John 1:3-4 (KJV) reads, "All things were made by him; and without him was not any thing made that was made. In him was life; and the life was the light of men." Everything that God created came out of Himself. He could speak, and things were created because out of Him came life, and even His Word took on life.

Interestingly, the Apostle John is writing by revelation here about Jesus' ministry in the beginning, as a principal part of creation with God the Father and God the Holy Spirit. God's Word took on life in the creation of the world, just as His word took on life when Jesus was born. I'm picturing Jesus, the Word, in the New Testament as the symbolism of God's creation in the Old Testament. As God spoke, the Spirit moved in power, and the Word manifested. What a model for His special creation—mankind!

"And God said, Let us make man in our image, after our likeness:..." (Genesis 1:26, KJV). "So God created man in his own image, in the image of God he created him; male and female he created them" (Genesis 1:27, KJV). This one verse should solve any issues regarding your identity. God did not create you to be like someone else. He created you to be like Him. Each person born is unique because we are created in His very own image. He didn't make any other species like Himself. But He especially made us just like Himself. We are a speaking spirit made in the likeness of our Heavenly Father. What He did, we were to do. How He spoke, we were to speak.

But sometime after mankind was created, there was sin and subsequent consequences of sin, which included the death process and the curse. Sin affected every part of the human race God created. It introduced spiritual death (separation from God), damage to the soul, sickness, disease, and mortality. For the first time, mankind developed a conscience and became aware of good and evil. The curse not only affected humans but the entire earth and everything in it, including the ground and all the animals God had created.

But because of the sacrifice of Jesus Christ, there is redemption available for the human being. We can once again fully operate as God originally intended Adam and Eve to operate in the Garden of Eden. And even greater so, because we have Jesus (the Word) in us, we have the faith of God in us and with as, as it was in the very beginning.

From Genesis to the book of Revelation, the entire Bible points us to Jesus—The Word. It points us to know Him as the living Word and as the light within us that differentiates us from the rest of the world. The Old Testament tells of the coming of the Word that was from the beginning, and the New Testament reveals the manifestation and fulfillment of the promised Word of our Salvation. In Galatians 3:16, the Bible also reveals Jesus Christ as the Seed of Abraham. When it comes to how things operate in God's kingdom, words are seeds. More precisely, the Word (the Word of God) is Seed.

Where do we sow the Word? Looking again at Mark 4, verses 15-20, it describes the four types of "grounds" where the Word is sown and reveals that the ground that the Word is sown in is your heart. Section 2 of this book discusses the condition of the spiritual heart in much greater detail. But here, it's important to grasp that the Word of God was from the beginning of creation, and God and the Word (Jesus) are One. Before time was—The Word was. In my eyes, this is a wonderful foundational truth. Every born-again believer must know the importance of not only the power of their words but their words related to speaking the Word of God as a creative tool and as a weapon against negative forces in this world.

It is also important for you to know that if you are a born-again believer, the kingdom of God is within you (Luke 17:21). If the kingdom of God is within you, that means you can produce kingdom results as you plant the Word of God—the Seed of Faith—in your heart. If you want to see the results of using faith, you must allow the faith of God to rise from His Word, which will, in turn, give you the confidence to know that God is His Word, and His Word cannot be broken. If God promised it, you can rely on Him to keep His promise because He and His Word are One.

When you think of the words "kingdom of God," it should bring to mind God's perfect design. Because words (and the Word) were in the beginning and were the model of how God operated in faith, this is the ultimate example of the believer's faith. God fully intends for you to operate out of your spirit and call things that be not as though they were (Romans 4:17). You do this by your words, by your command, by your faith.

Don't Drop Your Sword

The book of Ephesians is a book of the Bible written by the Apostle Paul to the Christians that were at Ephesus. He wrote this letter to encourage the Body of Christ to maturity in Jesus. It was written thousands of years ago and had key messages that speak directly to us in the modern-day church. As spirit beings living in this physical world, we must recognize that our battles are not of this world. Everything that occurs in this natural world has its origin in the spirit realm.

As written in 2 Corinthians 10:3, "For thou we walk in the flesh, we do not war after the flesh:" Meaning, there are spiritual forces behind every battle you face in life. So, the weapons we must first utilize to defeat these negative forces are spiritual weapons, not physical weapons, as you see in a military war, for instance.

The apostle Paul tells us what type of armor we put on in the spirit realm, as spirit beings, to stand against the devil's tricks and deception, who is also a spirit. Part of your armor includes what this entire book is about—faith! "In addition to all of these, hold up the shield of faith to stop the fiery arrows of the devil. Put on Salvation as your helmet, and take the sword of the Spirit, which is the word of God" (Ephesians 6:16-17). "Word" that appears here in verse 17 is "Rhema."

The Word of God is what you use to defeat the enemy. This is what you use to begin to plant the seed of faith in your heart. This is what you use as a weapon to defeat the negative situations in your life. As you utter the Word of God forth out of your mouth, in the Spirit, you are literally using your words like a sword to cut away whatever may be coming against you or your family.

Words can create, and words can destroy. Get a hold of this kingdom principle, and don't drop the sword of the Spirit—The Word of God. This is what faith is all about. Even when situations don't appear as though they are changing in the natural, you can stand in faith because of what you know by the Word of God.

As a spirit being created by and connected to God, you have the advantage of being able to use spiritual discernment. Not only is the Word of God a window into the Spirit, but God inside of you speaks (Word) within you. God will communicate with you, Father to child, Spirit to spirit. What a wonderful ability to have the Word of Life living on the inside of us! This is the advantage that we, as believers in Jesus Christ, have over the world. We are in this world, but not of this world. And God made this gift of salvation available to everyone who will believe in His Son Jesus.

You should be getting the idea that the most powerful weapon you have is words. It has been scientifically proven that even in early childhood development, talking to a child increases brain development. Words really do matter and are a vital component of growth and development in every human's life. So much so studies indicate that children without exposure to language-rich environments can enter kindergarten as much as eighteen months behind their peers. "Research demonstrates that the single strongest predictor of a child's academic success is not socioeconomic status, level of parental education, income, or ethnicity, but rather the quality and quantity of words spoken to the baby in the first three years of life[3]."

As a biblical principle, we know that words have authoritative power. What is being described here is a kingdom principle that deals with life and death being in the power of the tongue (Proverbs 18:21). So for those that read and study the Word of God, it should come as no surprise that words play a vital role in early brain development. Throughout the Bible, we can find very powerful examples of just how important the words we speak are.

Think about it from the standpoint of a marriage union. During a marriage ceremony, the vows that the bride and groom make to each other are declarations that they are making to each other before God and witnesses. In today's world and cul-

3   Why-It-Matters, Language Nutrition, 2016

ture, a marriage is considered a legally binding contract, which involves legally binding documents such as a marriage license and certificate. From a kingdom perspective, in the eyes of God, it's the solemn promises that are being spoken from the heart that makes it binding in the kingdom of heaven.

We are not obtaining physical marriage licenses from the court of heaven. As a spirit being made in the image of God, it's your words spoken in your covenant vow that God will hold you to. It's a kingdom principle that God sees as a covenant agreement between two parties, who are joining as one. Just as in the born-again experience, something supernatural happens in the spirit realm. The two are joined as one in holy matrimony of spirit, soul, and body.

As we will look at a few examples in later chapters of this book, when God made a covenant with man, He made it knowing that He would never break it. In biblical times, covenants involved a sacrifice, the shedding of blood, exchanging coats, and exchanging names. It had a spiritual root and could only be broken by the death of one of the parties. And the greatest covenant promise that God made with mankind was with the ultimate sacrifice of His Son Jesus Christ. He shed His own Blood and died for us to be redeemed, He exchanged His sinless life for ours, and He gave us His name.

We can see the Old Testament scriptures that revealed the coming Messiah. It was the prophets that were foreshadowing and declaring the One who was to come. These words spoken by prophetic revelation established on this earth that which was already written and established in heaven. In the heart of God, Jesus—the Lamb—was slain from the foundation of the world (Revelation 13:8). Which means, God in His infinite Wisdom, knew we would need a Savior. By His Word and authority, He spoke what was to be, and because of it, we have this free gift of eternal life. And the Bible refers to the church as the bride of Christ.

Words have creative ability. We see an example of this creativity and power in chapter 11 of the book of Hebrews. Verse 3 describes how, through faith, the entire world was shaped and fashioned. That is the amazing and awesome power of words. More specifically, God's Word, which is Spirit and life (John 6:63). There is only life in God's Word. This means you must take ownership of what you have created in your world with the words you have been speaking day in and day out. If you think you can just go around speaking idle words and have the same kind of results that only come from speaking "life words," you are mistaken and will end up sadly disappointed.

If you ever want to see results in the natural realm, you must first receive it in the realm of the Spirit. This may sound strange, but you must *see it before you see it and have it before you have it.* Meaning, you must conceive it and receive it by seeing it with the eyes of your heart for it to show up in your life. You must know within yourself and take possession of it (believe you receive when you pray) before you tangibly have it in the natural realm.

> *Life Application: Use your God-given imagination and see yourself walking in whatever you believe for. This will help you develop and shape the image of it in your heart, which is the fertile ground from which all manifestations flow.*

Walk in the Spirit

Believers must walk in the Spirit (Galatians 5:16-18) to be effective in the kingdom of God. God needs His Word—the good news of Jesus' death, burial, and resurrection—proclaimed to all nations of the earth. People need to know who God created them to be. Everything we learn in our formative years in school all focus on the physical part of us. But when it comes to knowing who we *really* are, who God created us to be spiritually speaking, it's often left up to the individual to figure it out. In the current culture in which we live, that can be influenced by the local church, social media, television, or within a household that is of the faith. Satan wants God's Word to be hidden, but God wants to make His grace known to everyone. This was the battle in the garden of Eden, and it persists today.

Light vs. Dark. Good vs. Evil. Truth vs. Lies. What side will you be on? Will you choose box number one (Life) or box number two (Death)? God has a designated path for each one of us. He designed a perfect will for your life, and He needs you to be in a spiritually mature place to receive what He has for you. When you are in a place of being led by your flesh, instead of your spirit, you are not in the position where God designed for you to be.

Just like with Adam and Eve, when they sinned, they immediately hid from God. Genesis 3:7 says that their eyes were opened, and they knew that they were naked. They were without physical covering all along, but now their sense-realm dominated eyes were opened, and their spirit-realm dominated eyes were dimmed. They made the first designer clothes (the Adam and Eve collection) made of fig leaves to cover what had once been clothed with God's glory. In verse 8, the Bible says when they heard God's voice, they hid from His presence, and then God called out to Adam and asked, "Where are you?" (Genesis 3:8, NLT). This is what happens when you don't discover who you are in the Spirit.

When the natural dominates you, the physical part of you, controlled by the negative influences and impulses of the darkness in this world, you are not in the position to walk with God nor operate in a level of faith that's pleasing to Him. God is looking for you and calling out to you—"Where are you?" You being in the right position in your life is not just for you to walk in God's fullness for your life. But there is a host of other people that will cross your path at some point that need you to be in place to help them get to where they have been called to be in life. The same is true for you as you cross the paths of others. God has positioned people to help you in life, those who God has prepared to assist you along your journey. That can only happen in fullness when we all are discovering who we are in the Spirit and operating as God intended for us at creation.

Don't be dominated by your physical, natural self. Who you are in Christ should dominate how you think and interact with the world. You must renew your mind to the truth of God's Word. If you are a born-again believer in Jesus Christ, your born-again spirit is full of the Word that was in the beginning. When you receive the Word of Truth in your heart and believe in the great Name of Jesus, you are sealed with the Holy Spirit of promise (Ephesians 1:13).

Start walking in your authority as a believer. Use the powerful weapon of the Word of God to start changing your world for the better. Become purposeful about what you are speaking daily. Allow your words to start working for you instead of against you. Believe God for what you need in your daily life and watch the fruit of it come up as you trust and rely on Jesus. Don't walk around another day as a mere human. You are a new creation in Christ Jesus. Take advantage of this new life Jesus has freely given to us who believe.

"Now faith is the substance of things hoped for, the evidence of things not seen."

Hebrews 11:1 (KJV)

CHAPTER 2

THE ANATOMY OF FAITH

Faith: The Life of the Believer

If Jesus is your life, faith must be your life. It's not just something that you employ on special occasions like when you need a new job, praying for a spouse for your single daughter, or help with breaking an old habit. No, faith is the life of the believer because Jesus is your life. And the Word of God tells us that we should look unto Jesus because He is the author and finisher of faith (Hebrews 12:2). Jesus Himself had to go to the cross of Calvary in faith, believing that He was the final sacrifice for man's sins and that His Father would raise Him up in three days as was spoken by the prophets. Jesus was the fulfillment of Moses's law, and by Him, grace and truth came into light.

In Jesus' death, burial and resurrection is our finished covenant promise of salvation (eternal life, deliverance from poverty, deliverance from sickness and disease, everything that we need for a prosperous and abundant life). The first step of faith for every human being is to believe in the precious Name of Jesus for the promise of eternal life. After that point, faith is a continual process and way of life of believing Him for daily provision as a soldier in the army of the Lord.

Like the military provides for those in service for our country, so too God will provide for His children. But God's provision is much better than anything that this world system can provide. We live in a fallen world with an overtone of darkness because the god of this world, Satan, is in a state of temporary reign. But as believers in Christ Jesus, we have the grace and the faith to overcome the attacks that come out of the darkness. The Bible says Jesus is our Light, which illuminates our hearts to the revelation of His glory. Faith is God's gift to us through the fulfillment of His covenant promise of Jesus.

> *Life Application: When it comes to the affairs of life, make a quality decision that no matter what trial comes your way, you will take a stand of faith and refuse to fear. No matter the situation and no matter how difficult, choose to believe that you have already won the victory. In Christ Jesus, you are a winner. To God be the glory!*

Three Revelations of Faith

In the book of 1 Corinthians chapter 12, the apostle Paul begins to talk about God's nine spiritual gifts. In this chapter, he reveals that these gifts are a manifestation of the Holy Spirit and are given and available to every man for their profit. One of these gifts, according to verse 9 of that chapter, is the gift of faith. The nine gifts can be divided into three groups: Revelation gifts (the word of wisdom, the word of knowledge, discerning of spirits); Vocal gifts (tongues, interpretation of tongues, prophecy); Power gifts (faith, healings, working of miracles[4]). In this article, Pastor Hinn describes the three revelations of faith as follows:

1 *Saving faith*—"that measure of faith given to every person" (Romans 5:1).

2 *Fruit of faith*—"an important part of the fruit of the Spirit. The fruit of faith is within each of us, as planted by the Holy Spirit,..." (Galatians 5:22).

3 *Gift of faith*—"comes for a moment, for a season, and for a reason." "The gift of faith is the instantaneous assurance of God's ability to act in a specific situation" (1 Corinthians 12).

I find it pretty amazing that the gift of faith is classified as a "power" gift. It speaks to the importance and significance of it, being in the same category as healings and working of miracles. Faith is a connecter to the things of the spirit, and it gets results! Saving faith goes back to us hearing the good news about what Jesus did for us when He died for our sins, and we receive faith to believe that we have been made righteous. Ephesians 2:8 (NIV) says, "For it is by grace you have been saved, through faith—and this is not from yourselves, it is the

---

4   Hinn, 2019

gift of God."

Within this chapter, I will describe in more detail the application of faith that I believe more closely resembles the fruit of faith, as it relates to the work of the Holy Spirit in the planting of word seed and the eventual reaping of the harvest. And as I will detail later in sharing my testimony, I believe the gift of faith was also in operation as God showed up in my specific situation. In that moment, I had no doubt about the outcome.

It takes God's Word on the inside of us to change our hearts to the point of unwavering trust. Jesus died and paid the ultimate price for the penalty of sin. After Jesus died and was raised from the dead, the promise of the Holy Spirit was fulfilled on the Day of Pentecost. All this has been made available through the sacrifice of Jesus.

Before Moses's law, the Old Testament believers, like Abraham, had the promise of the Word (and the coming of Jesus) as their basis for faith in God. We, as New Testament believers, have not only the fulfillment of the Word that became flesh, but we have the Word alive in us! No matter the type or level of faith we are operating in, we have the empowerment of the Holy Spirit, and we have been granted all the tools we need to develop strong faith.

The Holy Spirit moves you to hear and compels your heart to believe. Everything about our Salvation is a gift. What Adam and Eve lost through sin and disobedience, we got back in fullness when Christ redeemed us from the curse of the law. So, no matter how many times we miss it, if you're in the Son of God, all you have to do is turn back to the Lord with a re-pentant heart and get back in the grace gift of faith.

Faith Examination

To really understand the meaning of things, I like to break down its' parts and do a thorough examination of them. If you think about it in terms of biology, anatomy is the study of internal and external structures and the physical relationships among body parts. The word anatomy has Greek origins, and a literal interpretation would be "a cutting open[5]." I will use this illus-tration of human anatomy to examine or dissect the word faith to gain a better understanding of what Jesus meant when He told the disciples to "Have faith in God" (Mark 11:22, KJV).

But to do this, we must again go back to the origin of life, back to God's original design for mankind back in the Garden of Eden. As we proceed, this is where a few more of the orig-inal Hebrew and Greek words of the Bible will be looked at more closely, so stay with me here! If you want to live a life of faith and get it to operate in your life to produce results, you must understand what it is and how to operate it.

Let's start by looking at the word "faith." The word itself is primarily found in the New Testament. However, as will be discussed in the next chapter, there are many examples of men and women in the Old Testament who walked by faith in various instances in their life and saw God's mighty hand at work. This is very evident in the lives of those with whom God

5   F.H. Martini, 2000

established a *covenant*.

The majority of the New Testament's references to the word faith comes from the Greek word "pistis." This word can be translated as *persuasion, conviction, truthfulness of God, reliance upon Christ for Salvation*[6]. Conviction means a fixed or firm belief[7]. Pay close attention to the word salvation in this definition because this is going to be key to your understanding of a deeper insight of faith as we go forward. The word salvation is all-encompassing in terms of who Jesus Christ is Himself. Salvation, as either defined by the original Hebrew word "Yeshuwah" or as defined by the Greek word "Soteria," means all of the following: deliverance, victory, prosperity, health, safety, rescue. All these words describe the benefits that came as a result of Jesus dying on the cross so that we might be saved. We not only get the grace gift of being made spiritually alive with a re-born spirit, but we get all those other wonderful benefits that come with receiving Jesus as our Lord and Savior. Everything that we need to live a prosperous, joyous, fulfilled life is wrapped up in our "Soteria."

Life Application: If there is a lack in your life and you are born-again, you are not tapping into your full benefits package of salvation. The first step to receiving abundance is knowing that abundance is your inheritance and then using faith as the bridge to connect you to that promise.

6   James Strong, 1995
7   Random House Unabridged Dictionary, 2019

We can conclude from this short analysis of the word "pis-tis" that faith is specifically referring to God's truthfulness and our reliance on Christ, not a reliance or trust in our own abilities. Pistis is a person's total reliance upon Christ Jesus for every need or desire in life. This means Christ should be your source of faith. Another way to say this is that God's Word is the source of our faith because, as was discussed in the previous chapter, God and His Word are One. Just as God cannot be separated from His Word, you cannot separate faith from the Word.

Faith comes when Jesus comes. If you have Jesus, you have the Seed of faith in you. We can take the pressure off ourselves to manufacture faith by our own strength that we are not equipped with outside of Jesus. *To truly be operating in faith that gets results, you must be focused on Christ and not on your own human ability.*

You may be thinking, "Well, all of this sounds good. But how do I get to a place of having a fixed or firm belief and a reliance on Christ for the full package of salvation? I believe God, but I'm still in this situation, and nothing seems to be changing for me." If you're repeatedly speaking to that "mountain" of a problem in your life and complaining that it's not moving, you're likely doing it in your own strength instead casting that care over on the Lord and believing He's already taken care of it for you.

The Word of God has within it the faith to bring itself to pass. My prayer for you is that as you continue on this faith journey, the Lord will make Himself so real to you that you will have no doubt about God's plan for your life and His ability to take care of your every need. In Hebrews 11:1 (KJV), the writer explains faith as *"the substance of things hoped for, the evidence of things not seen."* The Greek word for "substance" here is "hupostasis," which is translated: a setting under (support); assurance; *confidence*[8]. This "substance" that makes up your hope is the confidence you have in Jesus, your reliance upon Christ for all that salvation through Him has provided for you.

You can think of it like this—faith is the support for your hope; it sits up under your hope and keeps it from falling. It's like the foundation of a house, an essential component to support the structure built upon it. Let Christ Jesus be the unbreakable Rock that supports your hope. Whatever that "thing" is that you are hoping for, faith is the support for it. If God's given you a promise, and you can back it up in the Word of God, you can absolutely have it if you believe you receive when you pray. Faith is the confidence that you grab hold of and don't let go because it's God's Word, and He cannot break His covenant promise.

Life Application: Faith is the confidence that keeps you in hope until the promise is manifested.

This kind of faith, which speaks of total reliance upon Jesus

---

8   James Strong, 1995

Christ alone, is the authentic Gospel of Grace and the free gift of faith that Jesus bled and died for us to have. I'm not describing a system of what the world will call the luck of the draw, or some get rich quick scheme where a handful win but the majority lose. Those things do not work in the kingdom of God because they are not based on Christ being the source.

Faith originates in the spirit realm, not in the physical realm. The Word of God, which is Spirit and life, is the source of our faith. If you are using your own effort and your own ability and yet are declaring that you are walking "by faith," it is unlikely you'll see the desired results you are hoping for. The world's system is all about taking a chance and wagering on something with poor odds of winning. In situations like this, you are taking a chance and putting all your money on something that offers no guaranteed security. This is not a very wise way of wealth accumulation and is not a kingdom principle that God designed for achieving success. This is not how to live a life of faith in God.

If you want to bet on something, you should place all your chips on the name of Jesus. There is win and loss in the world system of operation. But in the kingdom of God, there is only a winning side. That doesn't mean you won't face tribulations or trials, but it does mean you will always have the victory in the end when your faith is there to hold you up. The Bible says in Galatians 6:7 whatever you sow is what you are going to reap. The Word of God produces infallible results every time. The second part, Hebrews 11:1 (KJV), states that faith is also the "evidence of the things not seen." Your reliance on Christ is all the proof you need that your prayers have already been answered in the spirit realm, and it's on its way to manifestation.

Faith by Hearing

Now that we've answered where faith originates, let us look at how it becomes active and alive in us. As stated earlier, the Word of God (Christ) is the source of our faith. But how does a person use faith to the point where it is operable and effective in their personal life in a practical way? The method by which faith *comes* is by hearing and hearing by the Word of God (Romans 10:17). "Word" in this passage of Scripture references back to the Greek word "Rhema." You get the faith of Jesus by getting a word from God that speaks to what you believe for.

Hearing is so important to the operation of faith because it is a method by which a seed is sown in the heart. As I will discuss more in part 3 of this book, it has been an essential component in my personal faith journey. My belief for a new car debt-free started with me hearing a word of faith and ended with the manifested harvest of that word.

When you hear something, particularly when you hear something repeatedly, you start to believe it. Whether it's right or wrong, a root system begins to develop and what you are hearing starts to affect your belief system. If it becomes a consistent part of your thought life, it starts becoming a part of you. That's why hearing the truth is important. There are a lot of voices in the world today, but much of it is not based on the

The Anatomy of Faith

truth found in the Word of God. This is described in detail in 2 Timothy 4:3-4 (NLT):

> For a time is coming when people will no longer listen to sound and wholesome teaching. They will follow their own desires and will look for teachers who will tell them whatever their itching ears want to hear. They will reject the truth and chase after myths.

We want to make sure that we have the right influences speaking into our life.

I'm sure you have heard the phrase, "Knowledge is power." Taking it a step further, acting on that knowledge, and allowing God to give you wisdom on how to use the knowledge is key to unlocking the power. The more revelation knowledge you have of the Word, in terms of what Jesus has already done for you, the more life (or power) it will produce in your life. The knowledge that comes from the Word of God is not mere human knowledge. It will speak to your heart, the eyes of your understanding will be enlightened, and you will begin to receive revelation knowledge from heaven. This revelation knowledge will begin to be your guide, and it will give you insight into how to get everything you need for your life.

So, as you ponder over how faith has been outlined so far, you should begin to conceptualize why having the God kind of faith is vitally important. This answers the earlier question of not only how a person relies on Christ for Salvation in the form of eternal life, but how we rely on Christ for all that salvation brings (prosperity, health, safety, deliverance, etc.). Romans 10:17 in the Passion Translation of the Bible states, "Faith, then, is birthed in a heart that responds to God's anointed utterance of the Anointed One." In order to first believe and respond, you must first hear that it is possible.

The Bible is a book full of promises. Once heard, faith gives you the license to claim it and start believing for it. And as happened in my case, because I heard and saw what the Lord did for someone else, I believed it was also possible for me. Everything comes from something. As discussed earlier, faith is a substance (confidence). Faith is the catalyst that makes anything you can think or imagine possible. What is a catalyst? In chemistry, it is a substance that causes or accelerates a chemical reaction without itself being affected[6]. I propose to you that faith is like that substance. Once planted in the heart, it causes a reaction in the spirit realm. There is a reaction that is causing a production or a change in the spirit realm, and your faith is accelerating it.

Whatever you need, God already has it in abundant supply. You must have confidence in the seed of the Word of God that causes a reaction (formation of a new substance) that will accelerate the promise of God from the spirit realm to the natural realm to become your manifested harvest. I hope that you are gaining insight into this kingdom principle. When you grasp

9   Random House Unabridged Dictionary, 2019

the faith of God through His Word, you are grabbing hold of the very creative substance of manna from heaven and using it to create, or bring forth, what you need in this earth realm. That's huge! You can't use human reason to try and figure this out. Human reasoning is an antithesis of faith.

When you are hoping for something to come to pass, whether it's something intangible, like a better relationship with a spouse, or something physical, like a new house in a good neighborhood, you must give your hope the substance (confidence) that it needs (to survive) to bring your desires to pass. Hope needs to survive between the points of "I believe I receive" to "here it is!" Faith that comes from God is the key to actualizing what you are hoping for.

The Way of Faith

Since the Bible uses the parable of a sower to reveal God's nature and how things operate in His kingdom (Mark 4), let's take a closer look at the planting of faith seed. A farmer sows seeds in the ground in the "hope" of eventually reaping harvest when it's the due season. When a farmer wants to grow a crop, there are certain things that they must have to start the process. To begin with, a seed is essential, as well as a good fertile ground. Mark 4:14 says the sower sows the Word (Logos). Christ is the manifested Word of God. Galatians also refers to Christ as being Abrahams's seed.

As is outlined in chapter 1, words are seeds. So, when it comes to believing God for a promise, the Word of God is going to be your seed. If Christ is the manifested Word of God, we as believers in Jesus should be expecting the Word of God to manifest in our lives just like Christ Jesus was manifested when He was born into the world. Christ was born, and we beheld His glory. So too, the seed of God's Word that you plant in your heart will be manifested, and you will behold the glory of it.

The Word has faith in it to produce the desired results. Always remember that God and His Word are one and the same. To have faith in God is to have the faith of Christ. This is the way of faith under the new covenant that came by way of Jesus' sacrifice. The way of faith means you don't have to work for any part of your salvation. Jesus has done His part. Our part is to believe He's already done it.

When you plant the Word of God in your heart, you are, in essence, taking the seed that is already equipped with the faith of Jesus (Jesus Himself is the seed) and allowing that seed to grow and manifest a harvest in your life. Life is in the Seed, and the promise is already done in heaven. But to get it to manifest for you in this natural realm, you need to use your kingdom principles of sowing the seed of the Word to get your kingdom results. Therefore, when you are hoping for something to come to pass, the Word of God should be the basis for what is supporting that hope.

And what I find amazing about the Word of God is that it cannot be destroyed! The Bible talks about the Word of God being "incorruptible seed" (1 Peter 2:23). Incorruptible means something that is not subject to death or decay; everlasting. Christ Jesus is eternal; therefore, the Word of God is eternal. Before any of us were even born, the Word was; As we live now, the Word is; And after we leave this earth, the Word will forever be. The Word is everlasting and living. So, when we sow the Word as seed, we should fully expect it to become the substance, or life, of our hope!

Where do we sow the Word that we believe for? If you continue reading in Mark chapter 4 and verse 15, it says the Word is sown in your heart. The Scripture I quoted earlier about faith coming by hearing God's Word is one way you sow the Word in your heart. As you hear the Word of God, you are planting it into your heart. You can also put it before your eyes (look at it, meditate it) and speak it forth out of your mouth. It's good to hear the Word spoken or read by someone else, but it's even more impactful when you read it aloud and allow your heart within to hear the Words that are spoken with your voice. As a farmer needs good soil to plant seeds into, so the condition of your heart will be imperative to the outcome of your harvest. I will go into further details about the condition of your heart in chapter 5.

When you are operating in this kind of faith (the way of faith in Christ), you can have confidence that you *will* see what it is that you believe for. This is what differentiates those that are hoping according to the Word of God versus those that have a fleeting desire or wish. You may be looking at two different people who are saying the same thing, but only one of them is seeing the desired results. Both may be saying they believe God, but you must dig deeper to find out exactly what the person who is not getting any results is basing his or her belief on.

If a person is planting the incorruptible seed of God's Word in their heart, it will always produce results. If you say you are believing God for something, but are not seeing any results, check the condition of your heart. If you say things contrary to the Word, those words, or "corruptible seeds," are planted in your heart instead of the incorruptible seed of God's Word. You will not manifest all the benefits of the kingdom of God in your life if you are not focusing on God's Word and allowing it to produce undeniable results that belong to you as a believer.

Jesus—The Restorer of Our Faith

When Adam and Eve sinned, they did not only lose their relationship with God, but they lost their total and complete reliance on Him. The first thing that happened after Adam and Eve sinned is that they hid. They did this because they were afraid. Sin brought about the Spirit of fear in the heart of mankind and knowledge of fear that God never intended for His creation to experience. Sin robbed Adam and Eve of many things, but the greatest thing it did other than introduce death severed their unwavering ability to trust in the One who created them. Fear became the dominating force over faith. You cannot have fear and faith operating in your life at the same time. But what Adam and Eve lost through sin, we got back through grace in the way of the perfect sacrifice of Jesus.

The wonderful news about Salvation through Christ is that He has reconnected us to God, and now our hope has confidence because we rely on Jesus for total "soteria." Jesus was tempted at all points, yet without sin. Doubt and unbelief are both sins. And Jesus was presented with situations that tempted Him to do both, but He never wavered. Because of this, through His sacrifice, we too now have the ability to not waiver.

Jesus, who is our ultimate example of how to live life on earth, has restored our ability to have faith in God. And this faith, being a grace gift, means that in Him, all we have to do is receive the gift. The same faith that carried Jesus all the way to the cross, the faith that assured Him His death was the last and final sacrifice for the sin of mankind, and the faith that raised Him out of the grave, is the same faith that lives in the born-again believer. We can stand in Jesus' faith, and whatever we need, we can obtain it.

If we falter and miss it in any way when it comes to standing on a promise of God, it's not a concern. All we need to do is get back in the grace of God, find out what He says about what we believe for, and stand on the shoulders of Jesus with full assurance that God will perform His Word.

> *Life Application: The life of Christ Jesus is the example that every believer should and must follow to be victorious in this life.*

"For the Scriptures tell us, 'Abraham believed God, and God counted him as righteous because of his faith.'"

Romans 4:3 (NLT)

CHAPTER 3

THE HEROES OF FAITH

The Hall of Faith

Before we move forward to section 2 of this book, I think it will be beneficial for you if we pause to look at some of the biblical heroes of faith, particularly the life of a man named Abraham. These individuals have a mark in history as people who persevered and accomplished some extraordinary things in their life by using their faith.

In the Bible, Hebrews' book is often referred to as the "Hall of Faith." What is remarkable is that God chose relatively common people of their day who were from ordinary backgrounds to illustrate how one person's faith can not only be life-changing for that individual but impact generations to come.

They were not perfect, as no human being is, and may have faltered and lost hope at times. But in the end, what made them remarkable and worthy of having their story written as a part of biblical history was that they pleased God because they continued in the faith. They accomplished this, even though the promise may not have fully materialized during their life-time for some of them. God, Himself is even on display in this chapter, as He gave us the first example of how faith was used to create the entire world as we know it.

Faith is the kingdom's way of operating. It pleases God when you use faith to win in life, and there is always a reward to those who take the time and effort to diligently pursue Him (Hebrews 11:6). These are examples of Hall of Faith Heroes who used faith for the impossible. Each of these unique Bible stories would be worth looking up to see the full account of how faith was used to overcome whatever situation they faced. According to the following verses in Hebrews chapter 11, by faith:

- God: Framed (created) the entire world through the Word (verse 3);

- Abel: Offered God a more excellent sacrifice than his brother Cain (verse 4);

- Enoch: Was translated to heaven, escaping death (verse 5);

- Noah: Prepared an ark to the saving of his house and became an heir of righteousness (verse 7)...*We will look at Noah's life in a little more detail in chapter 7*;

- Abraham: Obeyed God, left his home and family, and went to a strange country he knew not of to receive the promised inheritance (verse 8);

- Sara: As Abraham's wife, she received strength to conceive and had a child when she was past her prime (verse 11).

Abraham's Justification by Faith

"For the Scriptures tell us, 'Abraham believed God, and God counted him as righteous because of his faith'" (Romans 4:3, NLT). This is how the Bible depicts Abraham, who to this day is considered the father of many nations and the father of faith. Abraham's early beginnings, however, were far from a life of faith in God.

Abraham (formerly known as Abram) was not an elite king nor a wealthy landowner but a childless nomad out of place known as Ur of the Chaldees. He was chosen and called by God to leave his home country and venture to a land unknown to him. At the age of seventy-five, this would be the first act of obedience and step of faith that would start Abraham and his wife Sarah (formerly Sarai) on a journey of believing God for the impossible...becoming the father of many nations despite being advanced in age and childless.

Get a picture of that. How many of us would be willing and then obedient to step out on faith in a similar situation? Despite the natural odds that were stacked against Abraham, God promised him he would make him into a great nation, make his name great, bless him, and cause him to be a blessing. God even went on to declare that all people on earth would be blessed through him (Genesis 12:1-3, Galatians 3:8).

Abraham's obedience to the faith was bigger than just him and his household. God wanted to bless the entire world through Abraham, and thus, Abraham's obedience to the faith connected him to God's great plan of redemption that came through his Seed—Jesus (Galatians 3:16).

Thousands of years after the time of Abrahams's life, Jesus was birthed, and the full meaning of God's promise to Abraham came into clearer focus. The plan that God put into motion to undo what the first man and woman did through sin, and death that came by sin, was unfolding as God purposed. Thank God for Abraham's faith, but even greater, thank God for the obedience of Jesus!

The good news for us today is noted in Galatians 3:14, where the Bible tells us that all the blessing of Abraham came on us through our union with Jesus through our faith in Him. Those who are in Christ are Abraham's seed and heirs according to the promise (Galatians 3:29). This truth is also confirmed in Romans 8:17 when the writer states that children of God are joint-heirs with Christ Jesus.

What precious promises are available to those of us who believe! Because of God's blessing on Abraham's life, he was a very wealthy man, to include the owner of livestock, silver, and gold. We, who are in Christ Jesus, have access to every blessing that comes with being kingdom citizens! Don't go another day without claiming what belongs to you as a seed of Abraham and as a joint heir with Jesus Christ!

Grace to Go Forward

While the apostle Paul preached about Abraham's justification by faith, it is worth noting that the New Testament history accounts of Abraham's life do not focus on his faults. The book of Romans gives the account of Abraham's walk of faith. Romans 4:19-22 (KJV) states,

> And being not weak in faith, he considered not his own body now dead, when he was about an hundred years old, neither yet the deadness of Sarah's womb: He staggered not at the promise of God through unbelief; but was strong in faith, giving glory to God; And being fully persuaded that what he had promised, he was able also to perform. And therefore, it was imputed to him for righteousness.

But years before the birth of the promised son Isaac (which was before God's second covenant of circumcision with him at age ninety-nine, where He changed Abram's name to Abraham, and before his wife, Sarai's name was changed to Sarah), the couple tried to help God out by taking matters into their own hands. Sarai suggested to Abram that he sleep with her Egyptian maidservant Hagar since they both knew it was in no way possible that they could naturally have a child in their old age.

Abram agreed to it. As a result, at age eighty-six, a child (Ishmael) was born to Abram through Sarai's maidservant

Hagar. However, God did not make a promise to give Abram a child through a maidservant. His promise was to establish his covenant through a son born to him through his wife Sarai, and this child's name was to be Isaac. So, thirteen years after Ishmael was born, God revisited Abram again to *confirm His covenant* with him and His promise to make him the father of many nations. This is when at the age of ninety-nine, God changed Abram's name to Abraham and Sarai's name to Sarah. Abraham was to undergo circumcision as the *sign of the covenant* God was making with him. Finally, at the age of one hundred, Isaac was born to him through his wife, Sarah.

What made it worse was after Isaac grew to the age of being weaned from his mother, Sarah became discontented with Ishmael and Hagar being around. She ordered Abraham to get rid of them, as she said Hagar's son would never share in the inheritance with her son Isaac (Genesis 21:8-10). This caused some agony to Abraham, because like it or not, Ishmael was also his son. But God reassured him that he didn't need to be distressed because even though the Seed would come through Isaac, He would also make Ishmael into a nation because he was also Abraham's offspring.

So, Abraham gave Hagar a little food and water and then sent her and Ishmael on their way to wander in the desert alone. When the water supply ran out, Hagar, not knowing what else to do, left Ishmael under a bush and went to a nearby spot to weep. She could not bear to watch her son perish. Ishmael also cried, after which an angel of God showed up to rescue them.

God then opened Hagar's eyes, and she discovered a well of water. This Scripture account in Genesis 21 goes on to say God was with Ishmael as he grew up. He lived in the desert and became an archer and married an Egyptian.

For me, the story of Hagar and Ishmael's life can be summed up in one word—Grace. God's overwhelming compassion for Abraham's son Ishmael was a picture of the Grace that was to come in the person of Jesus Christ. Even amid a family situation that was quite messy and I'm sure very emotional for all party's involved, God still showed Hagar and Ishmael grace. Abraham and Sarah decided to go ahead of God and take matters into their own hands. But God had made Abraham a promise, and no matter what happened in the course of his life, God would never waiver on his faithfulness.

The Bible says in Hebrew 6:13-20 that when God made His covenant promise to Abraham, He took an oath in His own Name. There was no one greater by which He could swear by. So God bound Himself with an oath so that by believing in His Name, all might receive the inheritance of His promise and know that He'd never change his mind. When God called Abraham, even despite his mistakes and shortcomings, He never changed His mind about him. Regardless of the decisions that Abraham and Sarah made, God still honored His word spoken to Abraham about a child being born of his wife, Sarah.

And in the hall of faith Scriptures in Hebrews chapter 11, what I find so beautiful is that God does not mention Abraham's past sins nor the wrong choices he made. God's grace and mercy are unlike any other. I'm sure Abraham felt redeemed by God's grace, as I did when God dropped these simple words in my spirit when I was dealing with regrets of my past—"There's a grace to go forward."

> *Life Application: If you find yourself in a situation where you made a mistake or have been hurt in some way by the hands of another person, and you've been struggling to move past it, know that God has made available for you a Grace to go forward. No situation in your life is beyond God's ability to heal.*

Referring back to the Scripture in Romans 4:19-22, God said through the writer Paul that Abraham's faith was not weak and that he was fully persuaded that God would keep His promise. This was a glimpse of God's Grace that would come by way of Jesus.

We, as Christians and born-again believers in Jesus Christ, would have the opportunity to have the end of our life's story be one of triumph. If you are a follower of Christ, the end of your book says that because you believed God, you were made the righteousness of God by faith. No matter what you have done in your past, in Christ Jesus, the only story that will matter for your life is that you were strong in faith, you believed God's promise to you, and you received your promise because you were fully persuaded that God would come through for you! Glory to God!

What's even better, we as believers in Christ Jesus have a better covenant than Abraham, with better promises (Romans 8:6). In Christ Jesus, all our past is erased from history, completely wiped away through the final sacrifice of Jesus. God says in Hebrews 10:17 that He no longer remembers our sins and iniquities. He sees us only through the eyes of Jesus.

God no longer sees you as a sinner but as a redeemed heir. The price for sin has been paid for with the precious Blood of Jesus. Abraham got a new name when God made a covenant with him. As believers, we get more than just a new name called righteous and redeemed, but we get a new nature, a whole new life in Christ.

Spirit - The Epilogue

New Life

Holy Spirit, breathe new life in me
In and around every part of me
Take up residence inside of me
A fixed position You desire to be.

Spirit of God
fall fresh on me
Where would I be
if Your Seed did not remain in me?

A cloud of despair
when for the body there is no repair
But Holy Spirit is in me
How's the devil going to evict me out of my body?

A spirit you've made me
The Kingdom of God is within me
When the enemy tries to destroy me
I say, NOT SO! You're not having any part of me!

A covenant you've given me
On the cross of Calvary
Blood on the mercy seat
Has solidified Satan's defeat!

72

Spirit - The Epilogue

Holy Spirit, breathe Your Life in me
In the situations in and around me
Faith in God even when I cannot see
Resist the devil, and he must flee.

Dominated by the Spirit
No flesh controlling me
Great will be my peace
His Presence will never cease.

God says, now faith is your substance
There is nothing too hard for Me
Come and have a seat with Me
A friend I will forever be.

———

SECTION 2: SOUL

THE PROLOGUE

Welcome to part 2 of your faith journey! Get ready for a dive into the soulish realm! I must warn you, though. This is the part of the journey you may find most difficult. This happens to be the part of us many struggle with the most. Why? Because of a sin conscience, this is where the battles of the mind happen. If you are not careful, this is where the cares of the world come to choke the Word and make it unfruitful in your life.

There is a lot of damage that can happen to one of the most precious parts of you—your soul. But don't be discouraged! The Blood of Jesus just didn't redeem you from spiritual death; it also restored your soul! And Jesus is a mender of the broken heart. If this sounds like what you've experienced in life, will you continue the journey and let the Father heal your heart today?

On this leg of the journey, my request of you is that you still your soul and mind and open your heart to receive what the Lord will specifically speak to you personally. You may find that some of what is said in the next few chapters may prove to be the most beneficial for you as you move past where you are to where you want to be.

―――――――

"Dear friends, if our hearts do not condemn us, we have confidence before God and receive from him anything we ask, because we obey his commands and do what pleases him."

1 John 3:21-22 (NIV)

―――――――

CHAPTER 4

The Anatomy of the Heart

Heart Examination

When it comes to humans' physical make-up, I believe God was very intricate and purposeful when He designed the human body, including the human heart. If you stop and think about how important your heart is to your life, it really is astonishing. The human heart is an organ that begins to develop, grow, and beat at a regular rhythm between five to seven weeks gestation. If it's in good condition, it continues this function for the duration of a person's lifetime. For some, this can be well into their 80s, 90s to a hundred or greater.

But that's the physical part of us. Because of the sin that happened in the Garden of Eden, every person born from the time of Adam and Eve would be subjected to not only spiritual death but physical death. Hence, this heart of ours will one day stop beating. But as discussed in section 1, if you are born-again, while your physical body will die, the real you, your spirit, will never die. Because of the sacrifice of Jesus, we have been given the gift of eternal life. And this is where our spiritual hearts come into play.

In the spirit realm, your heart is the center, or core, of your spirit. Just as your physical heart is one of your most vital organs, so your spiritual heart is an essential part of who you are. This chapter will begin by briefly looking at the human heart and how vital its function is to life in the natural. We will then cross over into looking at one of the most important parts of the "inward man"—the heart of your spirit.

Vitalness of the Human Heart

The human heart, which is part of the cardiovascular system, is the intricate organ system that includes the heart and circulatory system. All the functions of the cardiovascular system depend on the heart. The heart, which never rests, is the hardest working muscle in the body, and it supplies every living cell with oxygen and nutrients. It is located in the center of the chest and lies slightly to the left of the midline.

Think about how this super muscular organ beats twenty-four hours a day (approximately 100,000 times daily), seven days a week, for the entire duration of a person's life. This ends up equaling about three billion beats in a person's lifetime. The heart pumps roughly 8,000 liters of blood throughout the body daily. The cardiovascular system consists of a pulmonary circuit and a systemic circuit. The pulmonary circuit is responsible for carrying the blood to and from the lungs to be oxygenated. The systemic circuit, in turn, transports blood to and from the rest of the body. The heart contains four chambers, two associated with each circuit: the right atrium, the right ventricle, the left atrium, and the left ventricle.

The structural design and features of how God created our human heart enable it to perform its vital function so reliably. Just like any other organ, however, the heart can suffer a malfunction. Cardiac arrest, sudden loss of heart function, occurs as a result of electrical disturbances of the heart rhythm. If there is any substantial interruption or reduction in blood flow to the heart muscle, as can occur when there is an obstruction in one of the arteries that supply the heart muscle, a heart attack can occur.[10]

A New Heavenly Body

Our human heart is truly a remarkable organ that could have only been designed by a master builder. The same God that created the universe took the time to design a human being with such a sophisticated human body that was built to last forever.

As discussed in chapter 1, God created us in His very own image. We were not created with flaws of any kind. When Adam sinned, it caused death to come upon all humans. In 1 Corinthians 15:44, the Bible describes that there is a natural body, and there is a spiritual body. Genesis 2:7 records that God made Adam out of the dust of the ground first, then breathed into his nostrils the breath of life. But when sin came in, the spiritual death occurred immediately, which eventually is what caused the death of the physical body.

10   F.H. Martini, 2000

But the Bible speaks of how Jesus came to undo everything the devil did when he deceived man in the Garden of Eden. "For since by man came death, by man came also the resurrection of the dead. For as in Adam all die, even so in Christ shall all be made alive" (1 Corinthians 15:21-22, KJV). We had a perfect heart in creation and will eventually have a perfect heart once again with our glorified heavenly bodies. First Corinthians 15:54 reassures us that death is swallowed up in victory! Take comfort in knowing that faith in Jesus Christ causes you to win, even over death!

Life Application: When you are dealing with any type of physical challenge, whether it concerns your heart or any other area of the body, believe that Jesus has already provided healing for you now! Believe that you receive His healing power and meditate on what God speaks to us about our resurrected body that is promised to come: "So will it be with the resurrection of the dead. The body that is sown is perishable, it is raised imperishable; it is sown in dishonor, it is raised in glory; it is sown in weakness, it is raised in power; it is sown a natural body, it is raised a spiritual body..." (1 Corinthians 15:42-44, NIV)

Vitalness of the Spiritual Heart

What does the Bible have to say about our hearts when it comes to the things of the spirit? A lot! References to the word "heart" are found more than 750 times throughout the Old and New Testament Scriptures, with more references found in the Old Testament dealing with the wickedness of mankind's heart due to sin. I have realized in my ever-unfolding journey of discovering God that everything concerning faith, and really everything concerning the kingdom of God, is a matter of the heart.

The Bible tells us to be diligent about guarding our hearts because it will reflect what shows up in our lives (Proverbs 4:23). Think about that for a moment. Every issue concerning your life originates from your heart. If the physical heart is vital to our physical health, the spiritual heart is even more important to our spiritual health. So much so that our born-again experience is based solely upon what we believe in our hearts about Jesus being the last and final sacrifice for sin in receiving Jesus as our Lord and Savior. This, in turn, births the confession of our faith in Him out of our mouths.

Your spirit is who you really are and is the eternal part of you that will live forever. Your heart is a part of your spiritu-al makeup—your spiritual DNA. If God made us in His very own image, that means God has a heart. In the book of Acts, the Lord speaks of King David as being a man after His own heart (Acts 13:22). The heart of your spirit is what you want to focus on keeping in check as you walk through this life as a Christian. If that is in good standing, it will be the anchor that keeps you stabilized when things in life get out of balance.

From the moment you are born, many things occur in life

that will have a direct effect on your heart. Thus, there are a lot of things that you may experience as you grow and mature that you don't have control over. But as you get older and start making your own choices, there will be many things that you absolutely have control over. Getting a hold of God's truth is the only way to truly win over the negativity and darkness of the world that seeks to destroy a person's soul.

This is why the preaching and availability of the gospel of Jesus are imperative. How we show up in this world—the choices we make, how we respond to life events, the impact we make in the lives of those around us, and how we treat one another, is going to be a direct reflection of the condition of our hearts.

Heart Status

The Old Testament Hebrew word for "heart" is translated "leb," which means the feelings, the will, the center of anything. The New Testament Greek translation "kardia" is very similar, meaning the thoughts or feelings (mind); the middle. Just like our physical heart was strategically placed within our chest's center area when God created us, our spiritual heart is the very core, or center, of who we are.

The heart has been described as the seat of the conscience or the center of the whole person (Romans 2:15). Before there ever was the Law of Moses, which included the ten commandment moral laws that people are most often familiar with, God reveals in this Scripture that He wrote His ideas regarding morality on the heart of mankind. Romans 2:14-15 (NLT) reads,

> Even Gentiles, who do not have God's written law, show
> that they know his law when they instinctively obey it, even
> without having heard it. They demonstrate that God's law is
> written in their hearts, for their own conscience and thoughts
> either accuse them or tell them they are doing right.

People know instinctively what's right and wrong. Instinctively, in your heart, you know when something—whether it be a choice, an act, a behavior, an attitude—is leaning toward the "life" box or the "death" box.

When thinking about the sin in the Garden of Eden with Adam and Eve, I wonder why God would even put a tree there that was forbidden to be eaten of. Why even put something in the Garden that would be off-limits? Going back to the introduction of this book in talking about choice, and when looking at these Scriptures about loving God with all our heart, the tree of knowledge of Good and Evil that caused the fall of mankind came up in my mind. I believe when God had the idea of creating mankind, He didn't want robots as humans. He made us in His own image, after His likeness. He breathed into us the breath of life, and we became a living soul, with a heart, just like Him.

He wanted someone to love, and He wanted to be loved. As a supreme sovereign God, out of this great love, He had to give mankind the ability to choose. He gave mankind the ability to choose as free moral agents who were given authority over the earth. Just like our earthly relationships are birthed out of a decision of love, God loved us enough to allow us to choose whether we would love Him or not. We had a free will to choose to obey His instructions about life and live a life of trusting His voice on what to do versus what not to do.

Satan came into the Garden to deceive mankind into thinking they needed good and evil knowledge, and this forbidden tree was the key. But God had already made mankind like He wanted them to be, and with His guidance, they had all the knowledge they would ever need. But it was a matter of the heart, regarding which voice would carry more weight to them and who they would ultimately choose to obey. None of us want to be loved out of obligation, and neither does God. The same as it was back then, He still gives us a choice today. However, He will always keep His promise to never leave nor forsake us, even if we choose to go another way.

There are both positive and negative adjectives that the Bible uses to describe the heart of mankind. Some of the negative descriptions of a person's heart include troubled, hardened, sorrowful, evil, wicked, deceitful, blind, and haughty. On the positive side, these are the types of characteristics of the heart that God desires for His children: pure, sound, merry, honest, good, glad, trusting, single-focused, established.

People will often say of folks that are not born-again, "Oh, he's a good person. He'll give you the shirt off his back if you need it." But the reality is, a heart that is not surrendered to

God is inherently evil because of the nature that every human is born from, which is a seed of corruption. Good deeds don't get you into heaven. God is a God that looks upon your heart, not your deeds (1 Samuel 16:7).

Acts of kindness may be a good thing to do, but it's not the path to automatic entry into heaven. Only making Jesus Christ the Lord of your life makes you a born-again child of God, with the Holy Spirit moving on the inside of you, giving you a new heart and a new spirit (Ezekiel 36:26). Genesis 8:21 (NIV) reveals this truth about the nature of a heart that is not surrendered to God: "The Lord smelled the pleasing aroma and said in his heart: 'Never again will I curse the ground because of humans, even though every inclination of the human heart is evil from childhood...'"

These are just a few examples that drive home the importance of making sure we are regularly checking on the status of our hearts so that we are successful in our walk of faith and in our life as a whole. When the Father is speaking similar things multiple times throughout the Word of God, it will benefit us greatly to take heed to what we hear.

- Let not your heart be troubled (John 14:1, KJV).
- Let the peace of God rule in your heart (Colossians 3:15, KJV).
- Out of the abundance of the heart, the mouth speaks (Matthew 12:34, Luke 6:45; KJV).

- As he thinks in his heart, so is he (Proverbs 23:7, KJV).

- Trust in the Lord with all your heart; do not depend on your own understanding (Proverbs 3:5, NLT).

- Then you will experience God's peace, which exceeds anything we can understand. His peace will guard your hearts and minds as you live in Christ Jesus (Philippians 4:7, NLT).

- Blessed are the pure in heart: for they shall see God (Matthew 5:8, KJV).

- That Christ may dwell in your hearts by faith (Ephesians 3:17, KJV).

The Four Grounds of the Heart

In Mark chapter 4, Jesus begins to speak about the parable of the sower. He compares a farmer sowing seed in the ground to a man sowing the Word of God in his heart. It can also symbolize a person preaching the Word of God for others to hear and receive the Word as seed.

Just as there are four chambers of the physical human heart, this passage of Scripture talks about four different ground types or the four types of heart that the word can be sown in. The first type of ground is the wayside (verse 15). This type of ground the Word is being sown, but Satan can come immediately to take away the Word because it's sown in a ground that's too hard for the seed to be able to penetrate the soil.

The second type of ground is stony ground (verses 16-17). This would be like sowing the Word in a heart covered with gravel. You hear the Word with enthusiasm, but because it's sown in such shallow, stony ground, the Word is not able to develop a root. You endure for a short time, but when the emotions and enthusiasm dissipate, difficult or hard times arise. The person is immediately offended and loses the Word before it can produce.

The third type of ground is full of thorns (verses 18-19). You hear the Word, but the cares of the world, the deceitfulness of riches, and the lusts of other things in your life choke the Word and make it unfruitful. This is the one that trips a lot of people up because worry, which is sin and kin to unbelief, is the quickest way for you to short circuit your faith and negate the promises of God. The Bible says in Romans 14:23 (NLT), "whatsoever is not of faith is sin." All three of these types of ground (heart) conditions can cause a hardness of heart.

The last type of soil mentioned in verse 20 is good ground. This is the ground in which all the conditions are right for a bountiful harvest. You not only hear the Word, but you receive it by faith. This is clearly the type of heart you want to have and the type that God wants all of us to have!

In the following chapter, we will be looking at the "hardened heart," which the Bible makes a lot of references to. Just as important as your physical heart pumping blood throughout your body for nourishment, your spiritual heart and mind need to be cleansed and nourished by the Blood of Jesus. This is a daily process. The mind must be renewed continually in order for your heart to become established in the Word of God.

As mentioned before, we live in a fallen, sin-ridden world that is constantly feeding us information contrary to God's Word. As born-again believers, we must guard our hearts and minds against the influences that try to take the Word away when hard times come or that try to choke the Word of God through worries, cares, or the lusts of other things that vie for a place in our hearts. By faith, break up the fallow ground that may be consuming your heart, and begin to hear the Word and believe you receive it when you pray.

Just as plants draw up water and minerals from the ground through its roots, by faith, let the rivers of living water flow from deep within your heart to nourish the seed of the Word of God (John 7:38). Jesus is the ultimate Seed that comes inside of your heart at salvation. Everything else you need in life after that is born out of this precious Seed!

Life Application: As the apple of His eye, God chose you and loved you so much, He gave His Son to die to be reconciled with you. He deserves to have all of your heart, soul, and mind. Love Him equally with all you have to offer. Take inventory of the condition of your heart and develop a good ground where you can bring forth a harvest beyond your wildest dreams!

"Afterward he appeared unto the eleven as they sat at meat, and upbraided them with their unbelief and hardness of heart, because they believed not them which had seen him after he was risen."

Mark 16:14 (KJV)

CHAPTER 5

THE ESTABLISHED HEART

The "Hardened Heart" Condition

In studying the spiritual heart, it draws the conclusion that your heart's condition is not only imperative to whether your faith will be able to produce a harvest, but it is important for determining what type of life you are currently living. Before a person's heart can become established in God, you must first locate yourself and see whether your heart has become hardened to the things of God. There are several references to people having a "hardened heart" in the Bible.

What does the Lord mean when He refers to a person as having a hardened heart? The word hardened, in and of itself, can be defined as unfeeling, rigid, toughened, or unyielding. So, in the spirit realm, a hardened heart generally refers to any area of your life where you are insensitive, unyielding[11], or inflexible. If you are unyielding towards God in a certain area, you have a hardened heart where that area of your life is concerned. For example, if you know there is a matter that God is speaking to your heart about, and you don't give attention

1   Random House Unabridged Dictionary, 2019

to it, over time, you are building up a hardness in your heart towards God.

If there are other things in your life that have priority over the Word of God, you will be more sensitive to your life situations than you are towards the promises of God. This can be very subtle, but it is this lack of attention to God's voice to our heart that can cause us to miss what God wants to unveil in our life. If you relate to the natural part of you more than your spirit, you are not yet at a place of having a heart that is totally yielded to the Lord. In turn, what God says to you is not going to pierce your heart to the point where you believe it.

Don't Forget the Miracle of the Loaves

One example of people who had a hardened heart in the Bible was of Jesus' very own disciples. Mark chapter 6 gives the account of the miracle of the loaves. Jesus had performed a supernatural act that defied the law of nature. From five loaves, and two fishes, He blessed it and broke it, and it multiplied to the point of feeding five thousand men. By anyone's account during that day or this current one, that would be a "wow" moment.

After this event, Jesus instructed the disciples to take the ship out to sea and cross over to Bethsaida while he went into the mountain to pray. Night fell, and in the early hours of the morning, the disciples found themselves toiling to row the ship amidst a turbulent sea. Jesus saw them struggling on the sea, and He began to walk on the sea toward them. The disciples saw Him and screamed in fear, thinking they saw a ghost. Jesus immediately alleviated their fear by revealing it was He that they saw and told them not to be afraid.

He got into the boat with them, and the wind ceased. They were amazed at this and wondered how this could be. The Bible says they were amazed because they didn't consider in their hearts the miracle that had just occurred a few hours before this incident. This is what Bible records about that encounter in Mark 6:50-52 (NLT):

> They were all terrified when they saw him. But Jesus spoke to them at once. "Don't be afraid," he said. "Take courage! I am here!" Then he climbed into the boat, and the wind stopped. They were totally amazed, for they still didn't understand the significance of the miracle of the loaves. Their hearts were too hard to take it in.

Even though they had witnessed Jesus do the impossible in feeding thousands of people, when they experienced another problem while out at sea and Jesus once again came to the rescue, they were astonished and wondered how this was possible. They didn't even consider what He had previously done. The ground of their hearts was hard. Their hearts were insensitive to not only what Jesus had already done but to the revelation of who they had in their midst in the Person of Jesus Christ.

This truth is made even more clear after Jesus' glorious

resurrection from the dead. In Mark 16:11-14, the disciples once again displayed that they did not consider all the times Jesus spoke to them (whether in parables or directly) about His death, burial and resurrection. The disciples didn't believe Mary Magdalene when she told them that Jesus' gravestone was rolled away and He appeared to her as risen from the dead. Verse 14 says when Jesus appeared before the disciples as they were sitting eating together, He rebuked them because of their hardness of heart. Take a lesson from the disciples and learn to take the necessary steps to turn your heart back towards God. There is nothing in this world that your faith cannot produce with a heart sensitive towards God and established on His Word.

My Heart Issue

Many of us, probably all of us, have had our own personal challenges when it comes to matters of the heart. For me personally, I have made my fair share of wrong decisions because I never dealt with things in my past that negatively influenced the ground of my heart. While there were positive seeds that were planted in my heart, there inevitably were some negative seeds that came into my life.

Growing up, because I was not aware of the importance of guarding my heart, those seeds took root. Because I never dealt with the deep-rooted seeds that had taken a stronghold and corrupted my heart, I kept seeing the same patterns show up in my adult life. Different circumstances, different people, different locations, but the same story. The issues that I saw in my life forced me to examine the condition of my heart. As a result of really thinking about what I had allowed in my heart, the Lord revealed to me areas of my life; I had not fully surrendered to Him.

One such realization that I had to face was that I had a hardened heart in the area of trusting God with my body. This presented itself where both healing and purity in relationships were concerned. I also realized that if I didn't deal with this heart issue, it would keep showing up in my life and continue to lead me down the road of bad decisions and unwanted outcomes.

> *Life Application: If you currently find yourself in a pattern of behavior that you know is leading you down a wrong road, by faith, declare that the power of sin and its residue is broken from your life today. God's presence is with you, and He can and will empower you to make the right decisions if you consult Him and obey His instructions.*

When I have faced health challenges in the past, all I wanted to see was the physical manifestation of healing that I believed in. In one instance, after months of not seeing any results, I began to wonder why nothing was happening. I was using the Word of God to stand in faith for what is promised in the Bible concerning healing; however, I still was not really seeing the desired results. Like most people who pray for something and don't see any results, I began to wonder why this was taking so long. I wondered if my prayer was ever going to be answered. I had gone through a wide spectrum of emotions, from hopefulness and uncertainty all the way to crying with frustration because nothing seemed to be working.

One night as I was praying and crying out to the Lord, I heard the voice of God speak very clearly to my spirit. (God is a Spirit, and the primary way He communicates with you is through your spirit.) The words that He spoke to me seemed to come out of nowhere, and I was not expecting it at all. In the midst of my tears, I heard these words, "It's already done in the Spirit." I paused from my sobbing, not knowing what to think or even say when these words rose within me. I knew the Lord was specifically speaking to what I had been agonizing over concerning my healing, but that didn't seem like a direct answer to my prayer. In a practical sense, I did not know what that meant for me and how it was going to help the situation.

Of course, in my always strategic mind, I'm thinking, what do I do with that if I'm still hurting? I would learn later that *everything* that God is going to do for us, He's already done it. Jesus has already paid the price for my healing, and it's not something that is going to happen; it's already happened. Healing has a spiritual root. And even though my healing was already done in the spirit realm when Jesus sacrificed His life for mine, my current heart's condition was hindering me from receiving it.

Prior to going through this situation, I never really thought very seriously about the condition of my heart. I had heard the Scripture that speaks to guarding your heart before, but it was never anything that I put much importance into. In fact, I never realized before this that this was an area in which I had a "hardened" heart. I was not sensitive to what the Word had to say concerning my physical health. God opened the eyes of my understanding to the fact that I put more trust in natural cures and remedies over His promises concerning my health. I didn't make His Word a priority, and I considered what I was going through more than what the Word said about the situation.

God began to bring memories back to me concerning my early years growing up as a little girl when I would come down with some minor sickness like the common cold. I remember when I wasn't feeling well, and I was lying in bed, feeling miserable. My mom came in and prayed for me. I distinctly remember thinking something to the effect of, "I don't want prayers. I need some medicine!" Children are definitely self-centered, and during that time, I did not consider anything else.

Looking back, this could be considered an area where I started developing a hardened heart. I had never really heard healing being preached growing up, so as I got older, the concept of receiving healing through the Word of God was completely foreign to me. God can use anything for His glory and bring about healing in your body in a number of ways. This obviously includes things in the natural—through the use of medicine, surgery, and other therapeutics. Whatever you put your faith in and believe Him for when it comes to your health, God will meet you at the level of your faith.

For some people, as was my mindset at one time, seeking out a natural route to solve a physical problem is their sole source of hope. Doctors and healthcare professionals are needed in this world, and I believe many have a calling to minister health and wellness to the whole person, and not just the physical body. Many experts are now speaking more to the fact that there is a mind-body connection. But as believers, we also know that there is a spirit connection. And the reality is there are some things that doctors cannot provide a cure for. This is why it's imperative to know that you are a spirit being, and you have access to a healing source that was made available to you by Jesus.

So even if I decide to go seek medical care, my source and trust must ultimately be in God. The foundational trust of every born-again believer in Jesus should always be to seek Him first. When you seek the kingdom of God first, everything else follows. For myself specifically, because of ignorance concerning God's promises, I put too much trust in physicians. I put a level of trust in the hands of another person that I never gave to God. I've learned over time that this was imbalanced. There is no condemnation about it anymore because God has shown me this is just another area of my life where I needed to surrender to Him.

God is the only one who can do exceeding, abundantly

above what we can ask or think. The Bible says all things are possible if you believe (Mark 9:23). All things mean all things. Either Jesus died for everything, or He didn't die for anything. The Blood of Jesus wasn't just shed for our salvation from hell, and maybe a few easily curable diseases.

There are too many accounts in the Bible where people heard about a man named Jesus who could heal, sought Him out, and walked away completely whole. And on the other hand, the Bible also said that there were people who weren't healed because of their unbelief. So this tells me it's not God who's holding back on us. The "life" box is available, but are we going to be bold enough to choose it, even if someone else says it's not possible?

Jesus absolutely bore every grief, every sorrow, every sickness, every disease, and every pain that we will ever face in life. I wouldn't say this was possible if God didn't promise it in the Word. So, if something is not working in your life that you think should be, you should always go back to examine what's going on inside your heart, instead of thinking that God failed you in some way. If there is something that you don't understand, go to God about it with the purity of heart, and ask Him to reveal knowledge about it.

As I'm still learning and sharing in this book, I encourage you to go back to the basics and find out if you have a hardened heart in a certain area. Do a personal heart examination, and ask yourself, "Do I really believe God can do this?" An even better question might be, "Do I really believe God has already accomplished what I need in my life through the final sacrifice of Jesus?"

We are spirit beings who have a soulish realm (mind, will, and emotions) and live on this earth in a physical body. Our spirit, soul, and body are all connected and interrelated, and there is a very real connection between the three parts of us. Just as the Bible references, a house divided cannot stand. I believe that your house, your body, which the Bible refers to as the temple of the Holy Spirit, is sustained by what comes from your spirit through your soul.

I'm persuaded that God's provisions, mighty power, and anointing can only flow through harmony. This harmony only comes when your heart is at peace. A hardened heart is not a peaceful heart. God needs access into your life. Opening up your heart gives the Word and the power of God access, which begins the bring about real and lasting changes in your life.

Let the Light Shine

If you're not used to living life according to the ways of the kingdom of God, what you've read so far may sound a little strange or even weird. The more you seek God and His Word, however, the clearer things will become. What's starts out sounding foolish to the mind will become revelation to your heart. No matter who you are or where you are personally in your life, you need the light of the Word to shine in and on your heart. The more you spend time in the Word of God, the more you'll begin to know things by the spirit. Only the Word of God can open up the eyes of your understanding, so your mind can be renewed.

I believe it's possible to have a hardened heart in one area but have more sensitivity to the Word in another area of life. And thus, I began to understand why it was easier for me to receive certain things in one area (like faith for a new car versus faith for healing for my physical body). I had no problems giving or sowing, financially as the Lord placed on my heart to do. The Bible says if we give, it will be given back unto us. This is an area that I had a keen spiritual awareness of, as it had been a part of what was taught to me early in life. I believe with a sensitivity of heart in the principle of financial sowing and reaping.

As soon as I began to work in my late teenage years and into college, I gave at least a tenth of my earnings to God and saw many blessings as a result of this. In fact, my entire college education was paid for with the aid of scholarships and some financial aid, without me having to take out any student loans. Not only did I have enough money to pay for my tuition and books, but for my housing and a little leftover for any extra things I needed. Luke 6:38 tells us that we will get back much more than we've given if we give. I know without any doubt that this was God's hand that made it possible for me to finish college completely debt-free, without the pressure of having to pay back thousands to lenders.

Without even being very mature in faith or God's things at that time in my life, deep within me, I had the drive to succeed. And deep within me, without even fully comprehending how, I knew God was going to take care of me. Not because I deserved it, but because of His grace…His unconditional love that loves us no matter what we have or haven't done. Even to this day, I have many instances that I can recall that God has shown up in my life and has taken care of my every need. I give attention to this area, and as I honor God with my finances, He honors His Word, and the windows of heaven have been open unto me.

You can never out-give God. He will always give you back more than you can ever give to Him. The harvest will always be greater than the seed. I had developed a level of trust and confidence in the Word where my finances were concerned because I gave attention and priority to what the Bible said about giving. My heart was sensitive and open to receive from the spirit realm, and as a result, I was able to see my desired result come to pass. Had I given the same level of attention to God's Word concerning my body as I did my finances, my heart would have been more sensitive to receive from the Lord in that area as well.

The Established Heart

Now that you know what it means to have a hardened heart, let's look at how you begin to use faith to establish your heart to be in position to receive from God. "Established" means growing and flourishing successfully[12]. We have read the

---

12   Merriam-Webster, 2019

Scripture in Proverbs 4:23 that says out of the heart flows every issue of life. The goal is to have an established heart that is continually flourishing in the things of God.

It is possible to guard your heart to the point where you are in a steady flow of success. As you delight in God's Word, you will begin to establish your heart as a tree planted by the rivers of water that brings forth fruit in season. Your leaves will not wither, and everything you put your hands to do will prosper (Psalms 1:2-3).

"Establish" can also mean to settle in a position or place; to bring about permanently[13]. You can have a heart that is permanently fixed in the things of God and positioned to receive the Word of God. One way to establish your heart is to settle your mind by meditating and focusing on nothing but the Word of God. Focus on what the Lord has said about your situation, both what He said in His Word and what He has specifically spoken to you. In doing this, you are making a decisive dedication to choosing life despite the facts that may appear contrary to what God said.

There is nothing that Jesus' sacrifice didn't make a provision for. Keep your heart sensitive to God by not considering anything other than what He has spoken. The disciples had a hardened heart up until the time of Jesus' death, burial, and resurrection because they failed to perceive and recall the miracles He had done. They were distracted by the things of this world by being focused on the natural versus being focused on

13   Dictionary.com

the spirit.

Remember what God has already done for you in the past or what you've seen Him do for someone else. I'm sure everyone can think of a time something happened in their life that they couldn't explain. Perhaps something came through that you were not expecting; You survived an accident when all the evidence from the scene said you should not have made it out alive; You overcame a grim diagnosis when the doctor told you there was no hope. But it doesn't even have to be what some might consider a "big miracle." Think about anything that you know God did in your life when a new challenge presents itself. It's only in our eyes that we see some situations as bigger than others.

A terminal disease does not carry more weight than a broken leg where God's supernatural power is concerned. A $70,000 credit card debt isn't harder for God to handle than a $200 repair bill. We serve the God of the universe. He fed 5,000 people with five loaves of bread and two pieces of fish. Some people will read that story and think that it couldn't have been possible. Well, the disciples didn't think it was possible either until they saw what Jesus did.

When you see or hear about God doing something significant in the life of someone else, don't shrug up your nose and say in your heart, "I don't believe that really happened." That's the wrong attitude, and it reflects that your heart has been desensitized to God's Holy Spirit. He has a million ways to solve the problems that you face in life. God can touch the heart of a king for you if that's what it takes to get you what you have petitioned before Him in prayer. He can speak to people who are not even born-again, CEOs of big companies, to hire you when you are not even qualified for the job according to natural qualifications.

That's what an established heart can do for you. A heart that is single-focused on God and sensitive to even the little things that He has already done will open up the door to an immeasurable amount of possibilities.

When digging deeper into the Scriptures, another truth regarding an established heart emerges in the book of Hebrews. That truth is rooted in who Jesus is Himself—which is a picture of Grace. At the time of writing the book of Hebrews, the writer was speaking to the Jewish church in Rome. This letter was exhorting the church to maturity in Christ and a relationship with Him. Hebrews 13:8-9 (KJV) says, "Jesus Christ the same yesterday, and to day, and for ever. Be not carried about with divers and strange doctrines. For it is a good thing that the heart be established with grace;..."

The word grace in this passage of Scripture is from the Greek word "Charis." It is defined as graciousness, the divine influence upon the heart and its reflection in the life, including gratitude[14]. Verse 9 in the Message Bible translation states it this way: "Don't be lured away from him by the latest speculations about him. The grace of Christ is the only good ground for life...."

14   James Strong, 1995

Establishing your heart with grace means having the spiritual insight and conviction of what the finished work of Christ Jesus has done for you influence your heart to the point that it permanently settles you. Yes, you'll have challenges come your way that will try to test your faith. It may affect your emotions for a time, which moves you to want to focus on the problem more than the solution. But when your heart is established with grace, you quickly go back to the source of your hope, Christ Jesus, and remind yourself of what He's already done. The trial you may be facing is temporary, but the finished work of Jesus is everlasting and eternal.

This knowledge also automatically emotes a heart of gratitude for this free gift of salvation. A heart established with grace, in turn, is reflected in your life to the point where others can tangibly see it. Every seed needs light to prosper. Jesus is that Light, and He will shine His Light upon your heart. He is the same yesterday, today, and forever. A heart of gratitude should also reflect out into the world as graciousness that is extended toward others. As Christ has been gracious in what He's done for us, we should show that same grace to people that God puts in our paths.

The quickest way to get your needs met is to help someone else in their time of need. This requires another level of sensitivity of heart toward the Father, to hear and obey His promptings. You reap a harvest in the area of your need when you forget about yourself and sow into the life of someone else. Your heart should become settled when you know that the same God that worked miracles in biblical times is the same God who is showing up in the lives of 21st-century believers who know their God. Those who take Him at His Word are not forgetting the miracle of the loaves.

This makes for the good ground that this verse in Hebrews is talking about, and that is also described in Mark chapter 4. This is the kind of good ground that produces a harvest every time. Faith's role in establishing your heart to receive from God is anchored in the Grace of Christ Jesus. Once you get a true revelation of the fullness of what it means to have a heart that is established in God's Grace, everything else in your life will take care of itself.

As I conclude this chapter, let's take a final look at all three verses of Hebrews 13:7-9 (AMP) to give us a scriptural connection that bridges faith with the heart that's established in grace:

Remember your leaders [for it was they] who brought you the word of God; and consider the result of their conduct [the outcome of their godly lives], and imitate their faith [their conviction that God exists and is the Creator and Ruler of all things, the Provider of eternal salvation through Christ, and imitate their reliance on God with absolute trust and confidence in His power, wisdom, and goodness]. Jesus Christ is [eternally changeless, always] the same yesterday and today and forever. Do not be carried away by diverse and strange teachings; for it is good for the heart to be established and strengthened by grace.

When you are striving to reach a place of having an established heart, remember those that have gone before you in the faith. The most powerful example of faith is in the life of Jesus, who the Bible calls the author and finisher of our faith.

He, being all God, came to earth as a man to walk the path that we walk. He was tempted at all points yet did not sin. He had to have faith in God as He walked the earth and got closer and closer to His destiny. His destiny was one that involved a gruesome death on a cross. It involved being beat beyond recognition to suffer the penalty for the sins of the whole world. It involved hanging on a cross and being taunted and mocked by Roman soldiers, knowing He was the Christ, the Son of the living God. It involved ultimately conquering death, hell, and the grave so that we could have eternal life.

If your heart is not sensitive to the Word, it might be easy to overlook this powerful truth, but this was a walk that required faith in God. Yes, Jesus is the Word, but He was operating in the function of a man while He was on this earth. Jesus had to know, without any doubt, that when He gave up the Ghost on the Cross of Calvary, that His Father would keep His Word. There was no room for discouragement or doubt about His glorious resurrection on the third day.

But that's what sometimes happens to us at the first sign of trouble. And don't let a trial last for more than a week. Our whole world is turned upside down, and it seems like life is

over. We will never have to suffer as Jesus did, but the devil has a way of magnifying our problems to the point of thinking that it is the worst thing ever and we are the only ones going through it. Don't be carried away with strange teachings, like uninformed statements such as miracles or the healing power of God only happened when Jesus was on the earth. Forget that kind of talk if that's what you've believed.

Do you want to know why the Bible says there's nothing impossible for you if you believe? Do you want to know why Jesus said we as believers would do even greater works than He did? Because you're using Jesus' faith to believe for it! He was the ultimate example on the earth of how Christians (Christ-followers) should walk even when it comes to walking by faith. We have something even greater than the Old Testament heroes of faith had—Jesus Christ Himself living on the inside of us! We have a better covenant with better promises than what even Abraham had. And it is with that faith that He rose from the dead in victorious triumph, defeating death, hell, and the grave!

Before Jesus died on the Cross, He told the disciples that after He was gone, He would send a Comforter; One who would endow them with power—that Person being the Holy Spirit. In an even greater degree of manifested power, yes, faith is a gift made possible by our champion Jesus. Because we are of the glorious church of the last days, we get the privilege of living in Him and He in us.

Considering this, there is no excuse why you must stay in

a place of having a need, a want, or a desire from God. God has graced us and given us His very best. Look to Jesus—for it is the same faith that carried Him to the Cross of Calvary and established His heart to know His Father would raise Him in triumph, is the same faith that's in you today as a born-again believer. Take your Father at His Word and establish your heart in His grace.

There may be people in your own life that you have seen live a life of faith and that are flourishing successfully in life. I heard faith on a television program and said to myself, "If God does it for him, he can do it for me too." I didn't personally know the man that was giving the interview, but because I saw someone rely upon Christ for what they wanted, it inspired hope within me and provided a present-day example of faith I could imitate. God is no respecter of persons. His grace was sufficient to provide Abraham and Sarah what He promised them, and there are many examples to show that His grace is sufficient for us even in today's society.

The other definition of the Greek word "Charis" was graciousness and gratitude. This is a good reminder for us to remember always to be thankful. We should always have a heart of gratitude toward God for all that He has done for us. It's hard to have a hardened heart when you have a heart of gratitude. While we were yet sinners, God sent His one and only Son to die for us. I'm learning that whatever state of current affairs I find myself in, I'm going to choose to have a heart of gratitude.

Faith, which is the victory that overcomes the world, stands up against any trial or situation and says—"Whether here (on earth), or whether there (in heaven), salvation has come!" This means healing has come; deliverance, safety, victory, and wholeness in every area have come. No matter when or where the fullness manifests, the victory that keeps my heart established is the knowledge that I will see my salvation because it's already mine. And there is nothing that the devil can do to negate that.

According to Revelation 21:4, Jesus has promised us there is coming a time where there will be no more pain, death, or sorrow. God will wipe the tears away from our eyes because Jesus has won the victory over death. So, no matter where you are in life today, put your circumstances in perspective and rejoice in the truth of God's Grace. Let the divine influence of Christ establish your heart and put you in a position to receive anything you desire to receive from the Lord.

"Let us hold fast the profession of our faith without wavering: (for he is faithful that promised;)"

Hebrews 10:23 (KJV)

CHAPTER 6

Speak It and Do Not Waiver

Unwavering Faith

As you are meditating and focusing on the Word to establish your heart in God's grace, you must decide that you are going to stand on the Word in every situation and for every need until it manifests. The Bible tells us in Hebrews 10:23 that we must profess our faith and hold on to it without wavering. That word profession in this verse comes from the Greek word "homologia" and can mean not only to profess or confess but also acknowledgment[15]. When you are professing your faith (your reliance upon Christ), you are acknowledging that you are relying on Jesus because He gave the promise, and He's faithful to make it good.

The root word "homo" means the same. You are saying the same thing as God has said about your situation. In order for your confession to be the same, your thinking must be in alignment with how God thinks. No matter what it looks like in the natural, you're holding fast to the promise by consistently speaking the end result without wavering under pressure.

---

15   James Strong, 1995

The Stance of Faith

Many people often wonder how to stand on the promises of God when everything around them seems contrary to what they believe in. This may seem like an odd thing to say, but when you are walking by faith, it takes courage to believe. When everything in the natural appears to contradict the Word of God, but despite the facts, you hold onto your confession of faith without wavering, that takes courage.

Figuratively speaking, it takes little to no effort just to ride the current downstream when tough times come. To resist despondency and go against the pressure that's trying to take you down is not always easy. But every sound advice and wisdom that we need to overcome life's challenges have been gifted to us by God through His Word. There is nothing that we have gone through or lost in life that Jesus' Blood did not provide restoration for.

If you are in Christ Jesus, when the devil tries to accuse you of your sinful past, you need to say, "What past?" "What mistake?" "What sin?" All our past mistakes, failures, hurts, and pains were taken from us and placed on Jesus. He bore our sins and carried our sorrows. Don't let thoughts of failure and defeat torment you and dampen your spirit. God loves you. He is not mad at you for anything you have done or will ever do.

Every human being is born with the need for a Savior. In chapter 2, I talked about the Word of God being an incorruptible seed. Every person born after Adam and Eve was born

with a sinful nature, deriving from a corruptible seed caused by sin. Outside of Jesus, we were all subjected to eternal death due to our nature that had been corrupted by sin. We were no match for Satan in this fallen, sinful state. God knew this. And because of this, it was His love that delivered a perfect Sacrifice for the shortcomings of the man He created. Jesus is that Sacrifice. And there is nothing that we face that He hasn't already taken for us.

In hard situations in life, we must encourage and remind ourselves of this truth. This pain that I'm going through, Jesus took it for me. So, by faith, I give all of this to Him, and I receive my healing. Choose not to worry in the midst of your trial; choose the "life" box.

Forgetting the past can be a difficult thing to do, particularly if you had an adverse childhood experience that has impacted your life. But if you want to be completely free (spirit, soul, and body), you must let it go and allow God to heal your heart. You don't get a badge of honor from heaven the more suffering you go through in life. God is not in the business of making people suffer. The Bible is very specific on who the thief is.

Satan is our enemy, and his agenda is to steal, kill, and destroy people's lives (John 10:10). Our responsibility as a believer in Christ Jesus is to cast off every care. Cast every care and burden on Him because He cares for you immensely (1 Peter 5:7). The next two verses state:

Stay alert! Watch out for your great enemy, the devil. He

prowls around like a roaring lion, looking for someone to
devour. Stand firm against him and be strong in your faith.
Remember that your family of believers all over the world
is going through the same kind of suffering you are.

1 Peter 5:8-9 (NLT)

You have some people who have the mindset and belief
that they're just supposed to lie down and accept whatever
happens. It's the saying, "Whatever will be, will be." They believe that they have no control over the situation, so they just
stroll along and hope for the best. Some people are ignorant to
the fact that we have an enemy that is working against us.

When Jesus arose from the grave, He took back all authority from the devil and gave it to mankind (Luke 10:19). But
the authority Jesus has given back to mankind is only for those
who believe in Him and who enforce that authority in their
lives. You can't control others, but you absolutely have control over your life and all that's connected to you. The Bible
says we don't fight against flesh and blood (or natural forces),
but against principalities, powers, rulers of the darkness of this
world, and against spiritual wickedness in high places (Ephesians 6:12). You can take a stand in faith against any satanic
or demonic forces that may try to come against you or your
household.

Section 1 of this book looked at the Spirit part of us. The
authority Jesus has given to believers is a spiritual battle. You
have some well-meaning people who really don't cater to the

116

notion of believing in anything that they can't see, touch, smell, taste, or feel. This type of thinking is what the Bible refers to as being carnally-minded versus being spiritually-minded. It's another deception of the devil, as his motive is to blind the minds of people so they don't believe in a risen Savior.

Just as God is a Spirit, Satan is also a spirit. And Satan wants nothing more than for you just to take whatever unwanted package that lands on your doorstep without putting up a fight. He will try to send you packages of hardships, disappointments, and all kinds of temptation meant to destroy you, just to see if you will sign for the package. He will try to put roadblocks in your life to see if he can cause you to stumble or put thoughts in your mind to see if you'll entertain it.

If you are not educated about the truths of God's Word, Satan will tell you any lie to see if you'll take it. He's like a big bully. If you allow him to steal your lunch, he will. But if you stand firm and resist him, his only recourse will be to flee. You must enforce the will of God on the earth. Just because something has been promised to you doesn't mean it will automatically fall into your life. You must contend for the faith that you want to produce tangible evidence in your life.

In Jude 3 (KJV), the apostle John wrote that you must "… defend the faith that God has entrusted once for all time to his holy people." If you take a faith stand, God's Word will come to pass. So, fight to keep the Word on your mind and in your heart. Don't get weary and give up. If you don't, it will be impossible for Satan to steal the Word from you.

Believe You Receive When You Pray

In Mark 11:22-24, Jesus preached a message to the disciples about having faith in God. He said whatever you desire, believe you receive it when you pray. What this has taught me is that from the moment we pray, God hears us. We believe we receive when we pray. We may not always see the answer right away. Sometimes there are other people involved in your harvest. The reality is, most of the time, God uses other people to get His promises into your life. He may use one person, or He may move on the hearts of several people.

Just like salvation is a finished work in the spirit realm and available for you to receive from the moment you pray (believed in your heart and confessed with your mouth), so is everything else God has promised. For example, if you believe in God for healing in your body, as I described in an earlier chapter, your healing is already done in the spirit realm. When was it done? From the foundation of the world.

In the book of Revelation, chapter 13, verse 8, it reveals the Lamb (Jesus) was slain from the foundation of the world. This means God already had the plan of redemption prepared for us before we were even born. Jesus completed the work when He died on the Cross of Calvary. God knew we would need a Savior, and because of His great love for us, He purposed in His heart for Christ to die to save us from eternal death. When do you receive it? From the moment you pray, if you believe you receive it, you will have it. Your physical healing will arise out of your re-born spirit, where God's pow-

118

er lives.

Healing is a process. Sometimes it comes quickly, and sometimes recovery takes longer. Failing to receive healing or anything else God has promised in His Word is not about God withholding something from you. We, on the other hand, need to search our hearts to see if we are open to receive. Has your heart been established in grace?

As we looked at regarding the sower's parable in Mark chapter 4, when the harvest comes up, it's first the blade, then the ear, then the full corn in the ear. How long that process takes may depend upon many factors. We may not know when the harvest will show up, but we are to trust in God for the increase. But the key takeaway here is that it's already done! Everything God is going to do for you and me is a finished work. Trust God enough to wait for Him. The promises are already yours. That is indisputable in the Word of God. But if something doesn't show up or happen in the time you thought it should, continue to stand and don't waver in your confidence.

God asked me this once, "When things don't work out the way you thought it would, are you still going to trust me?" Psalm 27:14 (NLT) says, "Wait patiently for the Lord. Be brave and courageous. Yes, wait patiently for the Lord." How you wait is very important, and we will be looking at that later in this chapter.

> *Life Application: Don't ever let your outside circumstances dictate what you believe. God's Word should carry more weight than anything you can see, touch, feel, taste, or experience in your present circumstance.*

Don't Be Moved By Time

If you stop and think about how we live as humans, our lives revolve around time. We constantly have to think about when it's time to go to work; It's time to leave work; It's time for school; It's time to eat; It's time for bills to be paid; it's time to wait on the traffic light; on and on. It's the day-to-day monotony of our busy, hectic scheduled lives that condition us to think and center our lives around time. And because of this, it becomes a part of our subconscious and often becomes the driving force for handling every area of life. This is not necessarily a bad thing because structure in life help us maintain order.

On the other hand, I find this is why it's often difficult for those who are not focused on God and His Word to shift their thinking from being naturally minded to being more spiritually minded. When it comes to the things of the spirit realm, there is no time. God, who is Spirit, who lives in eternity, created us as spirit beings and has already made provision for everything we will need in this life.

As spirit beings who live in a time-based existence, conditioning our minds and our hearts to think beyond space and time requires faith. Faith is not intimidated by facts. The facts may be this, but faith says all things are possible to those who believe. I believe that faith, acting as a catalyst, can accelerate the time. But if you are conditioned to believe that something is going to take a long time, it probably will. Your ability to receive is based on your capacity to believe.

The born-again Christian is an eternal being who's seated in heavenly places with Christ Jesus (Ephesians 2:6). You were "born-again" into eternal life, and this literally means you have eternity living on the inside of you in your re-born spirit. You have dual citizenship; a citizen of heaven and one of earth. As an eternal being, time should never be a factor that causes doubt in your heart. The passage of time shouldn't hinder you from maintaining your stance of faith because, in eternity, it's already done. What we, as believers, must do is renew our minds to this truth and become more sensitive to the spiritual realm versus the natural realm.

Your soul must be still, trusting that God is handling all your affairs. Worrying is not stillness. Doubting because you haven't gotten an answer to your problem in three days or three months is not stillness. No matter how much time has passed since you first prayed to God for a need, as an eternal being, know that if God said it, He would do it. He had already made provision for what you needed before you even asked for it.

When a farmer plants seeds into the ground, he does not know the exact day or time the harvest will come. In the process of time, things will begin to happen in the ground that will not be visible to the human eye. When that seed is put in the

121

ground, it will begin to activate and go to work. The supernatural life force required for that seed to bear fruit is God-originated and God-breathed. Eventually, the farmer will begin to see small signs of life being brought forth out of the ground as the seed begins to grow.

Other factors make this harvest successful, like proper soil, irrigation, and sunlight. If the farmer makes sure he does everything in the natural to support a good harvest, he can rest assured that the process is working as it was designed by God to work. He does not have to go out every day, looking to see if something is producing and getting discouraged if nothing comes up in the first day or first few weeks. It will do him no good to worry that nothing is happening because time has passed, and he doesn't see anything.

Mark 4:20 assures us if we take the Word of God (hear it), receive it (sow it into our hearts in good conditions), it will bring forth a harvest. Once you plant the Word in your heart, you can rest! As you go about your life, not fearing or worrying about anything but meditating on His promises, watering the Word with your praise, you can be confident that the Word is working. You may not understand how, but the seed will spring up and grow.

The whole idea of the amount of time that has passed without seeing any visible results causes many people to faint before they see the end of their faith. I have had the same struggles in this area at times in my life. We must become sensitive to the fact that there is no time in the spirit realm. If God has given you a promise, if you lay hold of that promise, believe you receive it by true "pistis" faith, you can rest assured, you will have what you declare by faith. Yes, your faith will be tested and put to the challenge, but you have been empowered through the Word of God to stand until your harvest comes.

Consider another thought. There are times when you may have a strong desire for something, but you may not be ready or equipped to handle it. And then, on the contrary, there may be some things that you believe God for, and you believe with all your heart that it is time for things to begin to manifest, but for some reason, it hasn't happened yet. Regardless of the situation, seek the Wisdom of the Holy Spirit to minister to your heart about the situation.

If you're standing on a promise, I assure you Satan will throw every natural smokescreen at you to get you to doubt God and His Word. He wants you to be ruled by your senses rather than by your spirit. That is the only tactic he has to attempt to sway your heart from believing what the Lord has promised you. That is why it's important in the life of a believer to develop yourself in the things of God to where you operate in spiritual discernment.

You can liken it to an example of a package being delivered to you. It may be several states away and en route to you. But outside forces, like the weather or delivery truck issues may be holding up the delivery of your package. The package is yours, it belongs to you, you've paid for it, but you still don't have it yet. You know it's on the way, but some factors are causing a delay. There is also the possibility that negative circumstances have interrupted the delivery of your package.

In the technology age we live in now, and with the explosion of online shopping, we must be mindful of the "porch pirates" that are now stealing packages that are being delivered and left at front porches. If you are anything like me, if I know a package is coming and it hasn't arrived in the expected delivery time, I'm going to be calling or investigating why it's taking so long! I have a right to investigate to see if there something happening that's delaying my package that I'm not privy to.

When it comes to the promise of God, suppose something seems "delayed," just as with natural things, I tend to want to find out if something is hindering the arrival. This is where discernment and seeking the Lord are key. If it seems like a delay, I think it's the Father's heart for us to seek Him concerning all things. God may reveal to you it's a heart issue. You could be trying to manufacture something in your own strength instead of resting in what He's already done. Or He may reveal to you that you're verbally saying you trust in Him, but you don't believe it in your heart; no seed has taken root there.

Remember to examine where you are in your life, and honestly ask yourself the question of whether you are equipped, mature, and developed enough to handle what you are standing in faith for. A lot of times, this is not something that we think about at the moment. It's not until some significant time has passed, we continue in life, grow in some areas, and then look back and realize we were not mature enough to handle what we thought we wanted or needed at the time.

Or is it an issue of it being delayed because negative forces are at work attempting to steal or block what rightfully belongs to you? If the latter is the case, then thank God for us being able to pray in the spirit for what we don't even know could be going on! You can begin to use your authority as a believer to declare what's rightfully yours in Christ Jesus. If Satan is trying to steal, kill, or destroy your dreams or your promise that you know God has for you, your job is to challenge him and not retreat in defeat.

Referring back to the example of a package being delivered, what happens if you find out some porch thief stole your valuable items? I hope you would seek out the legal authorities to aid you in recovering your goods. Because a law was broken, if the thief is found guilty, there will be a judgment and sentencing for you to get justice.

For the believer, God is the righteous judge. Take the issue to Him, and He will fight on your behalf. I'm not going to sit by idly and let the devil or anyone else steal what belongs to me. In God's courtroom, you are always on the side of victory. But it will require a quality decision within yourself to choose to stand and believe God, who has all power in His hands, will enforce His kingdom laws that you declare on earth, as it is in heaven.

The Posture of Patience

One thing that I'm learning as I grow in more revelation knowledge and in faith is that you must learn the posture of patience. I know we don't always like to hear about having patience, especially if it's regarding something that toys with our emotions or is physically challenging. We all would love for things just to happen automatically, but that's just not how most things work in life. When nothing in the natural seems to be changing, this is where you must really trust that your faith is working.

I've been down this road before. To be completely honest, I am still being challenged in certain areas of life. The temptation to give up is sometimes very great. But it is in these times I remind myself God has given me a winner's faith. We don't lose in the kingdom of God; therefore, I refuse to be defeated. You must remind yourself of the covenant you have with the Father and know what you have a right to in the Name of Jesus.

Jesus Himself told the disciples to have faith in God. When you truly believe you have received what God has promised you, and your hope is now being supported by the confidence of the incorruptible Word of God, you don't have to be concerned anymore about *if* what you believe for is going to manifest; it's just a matter of *when*. During this process, just continue to thank God for what He has already done and use your shield of faith (as it is described in Ephesians 6:16) to come against any mind games that may come to deter you or cause you to doubt when times get hard.

Several Bible verses speak to the importance of having patience when it comes to believing for the promises of God. We looked at the example of Abraham's life and how after he patiently waited, the Bible says he received the promise (Hebrews 6:15). Even concerning the return of Jesus, the Bible records that no one knows the day nor the hour (Matthew 24:36; 24:44; Mark 13:32). But we look for Him because we know He's coming. As Christians, we are patiently and expectantly waiting for His return.

So too, we may not know the day or the hour when the Word of God or a promise will show up in our life, but we look for it because we know it's coming. What should the posture of your patience be while you wait? How does patience look from a practical standpoint? These are some simple points and a few reminders that God has revealed to me about how we as believers should be standing in faith.

1. **Speak only what God says.** No matter what the situation looks like, you must determine in your heart to only speak what God has spoken, and focus on the answer and not the problem. Don't let the temporary interrupt your eternal. The Bible declares in 2 Corinthians 4:18 (NLT), "So we don't look at the troubles we can see now; rather, we fix our gaze on things that cannot be seen. For the things we see now will soon be gone, but the things we cannot see will last forever."

2. **Actively resist.** If you submit yourself to God and re-

sist the devil and all his attacks, the Bible says Satan will flee away from you (James 4:7). If it's a sickness that is coming against your body, submit to God's authority and His will concerning your healing, and then actively resist the sickness in the Name of Jesus by boldly declaring you are healed by the stripes of Jesus. If it's a spirit of depression that you are dealing with, get God's Word that speaks to positive emotions like joy and peace, and actively resist the spirit of depression that's trying to overwhelm you. Use the Word of God as a source of light to shine upon the darkness of depressive thoughts. Again, words have power. By simply speaking the Word of God, you will counteract negative thought patterns and will begin to shift things in the spirit realm. God is a loving Father and is always at our aid to lead, guide, and comfort us when we're under attack.

3. **Keep your heart sensitive.** Consider the Word of God more than you consider the problem. Take time to meditate on the Word of God daily until it becomes more real to you than your problem. This will require a level of commitment on your part to remain consistent. As was stated in an earlier chapter, keep your heart sensitive by remembering what God has already done. If nothing else, remember that God provided a sacrifice to free you from sin and all its consequences. Meditating on His goodness and putting yourself

in remembrance of this one thing alone will shift you into a place of victory no matter what chaos is going on around you. "But they delight in the law of the Lord, meditating on it day and night" (Psalm 1:2 NLT).

4. **Be still and know**. The Lord says to us in Psalm 46:10 (KJV), "Be still, and know that I am God." Worry, doubt, and fear are all enemies of the faith. You are not at rest, trusting God to take care of you if you have no peace in your soul. If you are a person that worries about everything, your meditation should be Matthew 6:25-34. Here in this passage, Jesus teaches why worrying will do you no good in life. You will not add anything good to your life by living with a fearful heart. Seek God first above all, quiet your mind and heart, and wait for the Lord to speak to you about your life. Stop worrying about tomorrow and thank God for what you have today. Be still and know that God is your Father, and He will take care of you.

5. **Wait upon the Lord.** Isaiah 40:31 (KJV) says, "But they that wait upon the Lord shall renew their strength; they shall mount up with wings as eagles; they shall run, and not be weary, and they shall walk, and not faint." Waiting upon the Lord is not an excuse to be complacent, and it doesn't mean to tolerate or put up with something. Your posture should be one of eager expectation, knowing in your heart, your answer is on

the way. Being consistent about what you are speaking and believing is the posture of patience. This confident expectation exemplifies your trust in Him, your rest in Him, and your reliance on Him as your God, who is able to take care of all of your wants and needs.

Beautiful In Its Time

The Bible states in Ecclesiastes 3:1-2 (KJV), "To every thing there is a season, and a time to every purpose under the heaven: A time to be born, and a time to die; a time to plant, and a time to pluck up that which is planted;" Another reason why we don't have to be moved by time is that God has told us that times and seasons are a part of life. Similar to the situation describing the farmer planting the seed and waiting for the harvest, we do know that there are other parts of our life in the natural where the passing of time is needed for growth and maturity.

In medical science, when a woman conceives and becomes pregnant, her baby is considered to be full-term between thirty-nine and forty weeks gestation. It is the optimal amount of time a baby needs to grow and develop before being fully prepared to be born and survive outside the womb. There are risks to a baby's health when born prematurely because they are not yet fully developed in all areas.

I think the same thing is true for us spiritually. When we take God's Word into our hearts like a seed, we are growing even as the seed is growing in us. We are becoming more confident in the Word. Growth and development are also preparing us to be fully equipped to enter into that season where God's promise is birthed in our life.

An example of this is a person that has a desire to be a millionaire. Let's say this person is not good with money management, has a spending habit, and is in large financial debt because of this habit. Becoming a millionaire at that time would not be in that person's best interest. If you are a person who can't manage $30,000, you will not be able to manage a million.

An opposing argument would be, well, the person can get a financial advisor. This is true, and a financial advisor can guide you into ways to invest and manage your newfound wealth, but the person who has the wealth is ultimately in control and responsible for how it's handled. If you had a spending problem before you came into a lot of money, you would still have the same spending problem after you get the money if you do not deal with the root issue.

In this instance, time to allow for growth and maturity is a protective factor for this person. Taking the time to learn better spending habits and money management skills with the current income they have will better equip a person to handle the greater wealth they desire to come into their lives.

Parts of our faith journey in life will require some good sneakers because there will be some roads that will require us to walk it out. And we should be prepared that some parts of this path will be an uphill climb. There is a process for most things in life. For certain things, the process could be sudden or immediate, but it may be more gradual for other things.

During the time of Jesus' life here on earth, there were all types of people He encountered who came to Him with a multitude of problems. The Bible describes various accounts of people who sought Him out for healing. Some manifestations happened immediately; some things happened within the same hour; some accounts even said as they went, they were healed. The important point here is that no matter the time, healing came to those who believed.

The Bible tells us that as long as the earth remains, there will be seedtime and harvest (Genesis 8:22, KJV). I know enough to know that planting the Word of God in your heart works. This is a good starting place. So don't be discouraged if you don't see immediate results. Start where you are in your faith walk and believe God that your faith will grow stronger and stronger as you walk with Him. We can be confident that if we are putting our trust in God, who has already done the Work, we will see the end of our faith.

No matter what time or season of life you are in, I encourage you to start enjoying the journey today. Even if some parts of your road get a little bumpy, you have eternity on the inside of you! If there is weeping and mourning today, there could very well be joy and laughter awaiting in your tomorrow. Have faith for God to show up and show out in your life, even as you remember He is with you always.

Life Application: Meditate on these words whenever you feel discouraged about where you are in your life: "He has made everything beautiful in its time. He has also set eternity in the human heart; yet no one can fathom what God has done from beginning to end. I know that there is nothing better for people than to be happy and to do good while they live" (Ecclesiastes 3:11-12, NIV).

SOUL - THE EPILOGUE

THE FINAL HOUR

In this final hour
Let your hope remain in Me
What others couldn't see
Be assured you are about to see

Continue to trust in Me
Don't let pressure enter thee
With your heart, you believe
With your heart, you will receive

Faith in your heart
Word in your mouth
Established in the Blood
Anchored from the flood

Let this quiet confidence
Prove to be your reward
In My Word, there is no lack
The Great I AM is coming back

Your good ground
Is now ripe for harvest
I've answered your heart
And it will never depart

Take your place, my child
Upon the Father's faithful hand
Now established in My grace
Your final hour is My resting place

———

SECTION 3: BODY

THE PROLOGUE

Wow...you have made it to the last leg of your faith journey! This is where we go from "I believe I receive" to "Here it is!" If you have sought first the kingdom of God and his righteousness, you can rest assured that everything you need is about to manifest (Matthew 6:33).

The three parts of faith's journey are laid out in order of priority. If you have obtained a promise from the Spirit of God, planted it in your heart, and have allowed God to restore your soul, your confident expectation is about to yield extraordinary results! Bringing in the harvest does require action on your part, but this will be a labor of love that will mark your life forever.

Hence, the "body" in the final hour of your faith journey represents anything in your physical world that you need to manifest for yourself. This includes things such as physical or emotional healing, deliverance from a bad habit or addiction, restored relationships, the job of your dreams, or possibly the mate of your dreams! You get the idea. This faith journey was designed to get results. What good is it, after all, if it forever remains just a hope?

"And as soon as the grain is ready, the farmer comes and harvests it with a sickle, for the harvest time has come."

Mark 4:29 (NLT)

CHAPTER 7

———

HARVEST TIME

Your Harvest is Coming!

Mark 4:29 talks about the harvest being brought forth. In that same chapter, Jesus also says there is nothing hid (unseen) that will not eventually be made manifest (seen). This gives me much confidence in knowing that your harvest, whatever you believe God for, will come! But for this to happen, you must adhere to the earlier chapter that discussed the ground's condition (your spiritual heart). This will inevitably have a direct impact on your harvest.

My maternal grandfather, Henry Peter Bennett, who was affectionately known to many as "Son," was a very humble man. He worked a blue-collar job for many years but was also a farmer at heart. Growing up, I would watch him as he planted vegetable seeds in his garden. All the southern favorites he planted, like sweet potatoes, collard greens, and okra, he would share with others. It was a joy for him. Sowing seeds, knowing the harvest that it would yield, was an act of love for him.

I was much too young at the time to appreciate all that went into preparing the ground before the planting of the seeds, but he was diligent at what he did. Just as he was a diligent farmer, he had to be a diligent reaper. When you sow seeds, you should expect a harvest. My grandfather made sure all the elements he could control in the natural were done with precision. Everything else, he trusted in the Lord to bring the increase.

My grandfather was an early riser, and on September 9th, 2016, he saw the sunrise for the very last time on this side of heaven. His spirit left his body, and he went home to be with the Lord. Some months before he passed away, he was out in his field doing what he loved to do, planting seeds. It wasn't until his funeral that I thought about something as a deacon at the church recounted his memories of my grandfather.

He talked about how Mr. Bennett loved being out in his field, but what he may or may not have had an awareness of at the time is that the harvest from the seeds he planted would have to be gathered by someone else. My youngest brother was sitting next to me, and for some reason, he started to cry after hearing those words. I hadn't thought of that before, but it rang so true to me when I heard it.

We are often tunnel-visioned when we are working our plans, sowing seeds in our lives, and believing God for a promise to come to pass; however, many of us fail to realize that God's plans are always bigger than ours.

The kingdom of God is all about seed, time, and harvest.

It's about a person planting a seed in the ground, sleeping and rising night and day, and that seed springing up and growing without him even knowing how. That's the kingdom principle of how everything in life operates. The earth will bring forth the fruit of herself. Our job is to work the process. If you're consistently sowing, you should consistently be reaping the benefits of your seeds sown.

The lesson my grandfather exemplified at the end of his life here on earth was that even if you are not here to see it, your harvest is coming! The time, effort, and love that you put into sowing and nurturing a seed may eventually be for the benefit of someone else.

This same sentiment is expressed in Hebrews 11, as the writer describes the faith of the Patriarchs of the Old Testament: "These heroes all died still clinging to their faith, not even receiving all that had been promised them. But they saw beyond the horizon the fulfillment of their promise and gladly embraced it from afar. They all lived their lives on earth as those who belonged to another realm" (Hebrews 11:13, TPT).

The Wait is Over

It was Labor Day weekend, Saturday, August 30th, 2008, when I found myself standing amongst onlookers, dealership employees, the media, and a crowd of eager contestant hopefuls. Each contestant was randomly selected as one of several finalists in a car dealership contest called "Keys to Summer Savings Car Giveaway."

I was in the crowd as one of those anxious contestant finalists. How I arrived at becoming a finalist was nothing short of divine. It was not something I could have dreamt up on my own or even written a better script for. This was one scene that I like to say came straight out of heaven's playbook.

On the contrary, how I literally arrived at the location was in an old 1996 Nissan Sentra that had well over 200,000 miles on it. As I drove to the dealership that day, I knew I would be calling someone to come and drive my old car home for me. I had indescribable confidence within me that assured me this was the day my faith was going to produce the manifestation of my hope.

The rules of the contest were simple. When your name was called, you were to pick only one of the several blank CDs laid out on the table and then insert it into the car CD player. If you heard the sound of a horn, that meant you didn't win. But if you heard the sound of an engine starting, well, you probably can guess what that sound meant! That's the sound everyone was eager to hear because that meant you had chosen the right CD, and you were the winner.

There were a few names called before mine. I didn't count the number exactly, but I would say about ten or so. As each person one by one inserted their CD into the car's CD player, we all kept hearing the sound of the horn. When my name was called, I approached the table to see there were still a lot of blank CDs left to choose from. At that moment, I just softly spoke to God within myself and said something to the effect of

"Okay, God, which one of these is the right one?"

I did not hear an audible voice, nor did I specifically hear God's voice within my spirit giving me specific instructions about which row or spot the correct CD was in. What I did have was an inward witness of which to choose. This is where I believe the gift of faith was in operation as the Holy Spirit manifested His power in me.

The power of God showed up at this moment and gave me an instantaneous assurance that He was with me and was going to act on my behalf to give me the victory. Through this assurance on the inside, the Lord gave me the thought about where to look. I acknowledged Him, and as a result, I chose the "life" box (Proverbs 3:5-6). The moment I asked the Father for direction, I felt a prompting that shifted my gaze to the right side of the table.

After just a few seconds of standing there, I stretched forth my hand by faith and chose the farthest CD on the right side of the table on the top row. I wasn't looking for a feeling or an emotion, but I simply believed that He would direct me. I took the CD I had chosen, approached the car, and sat in the driver's seat. After inserting my CD in the player, guess what the sound was that everyone heard? There was a slight pause...(which was different than the immediate horn which was heard for several contestants before me), and then the sound of an engine revving! Glory to God! The Lord had brought His Word to pass!

143

I can't even fully express to you how I felt on the inside at that moment. A flood of tears began to well and cascade from my eyes. As you can imagine, cameras were in my face catching the moment, and there were loads of strangers staring at me and clapping in applause. But despite all this flurry of activity, everything in that moment became silent, and my surroundings ceased to exist. An overwhelming sense of God's love flooded my heart.

Even though leading up to this point, I knew this was the day God was going to answer my heart; still, in that very moment, I was so amazed at just how very purposeful my God is. For months I held onto a promise. The many days of meditating and envisioning myself with a new car, intentional and heartfelt thanksgiving and praising God for what He had already done even before it manifested, had all culminated in this one moment of time. God did exactly what I asked...just like I asked Him. I did not know how or when, but I believed.

Looking back on this time, what I find truly amazing is all the factors that had to come together for me to come into the fulfillment of this promise. While I was oblivious to what was happening in the spirit realm, God was orchestrating this plan and giving the owner of a dealership a thought about having a contest. All of this was the foundation for what I needed to be manifested in this natural realm.

This is not something I could have done in my own ability if I wanted it supernaturally. In my own ability, I only had the means to finance a car and be in debt to a lender. However, if I wanted it supernaturally, I needed God's help. What God needed from me was for me to operate His kingdom principle for the manifestation of kingdom results. He needed a seed.

What began in my imagination as hope had to turn into faith by what I believed according to God's Word. As discussed in section 1, faith comes from hearing and believing the Word of God. Once I got a hold of God's Word, my hope now had substance, which produces results every time. Everything we need has already been provided for us by our Heavenly Father. Your faith will bring about the desired manifestation.

When you operate in faith, you are using the supernatural seed of God's Word to produce supernatural results in this natural world. One definition of the word supernatural is "of, relating to, or being above or beyond what is natural; unexplainable by natural law or phenomena."[16] When you are operating in faith, you are not operating in natural law, like the law of gravity, for instance. Faith is a higher law. If it worked for those faith heroes in the Old Testament, if it worked for Jesus who was raised from the dead, and if it worked for this born-again believer from a little country town in South Carolina, it will work for you too!

Trust in the "Not Knowing"

One thing I know for sure about believing God for a new car is that I did not get caught up in the details. Because I am a very detailed oriented person, I most often refer to this situation to

---

16   Harper, 2010

remind myself of this key point. If you start getting caught up in trying to figure out every little detail of how something will work—before you just believe it because God said it—you'll miss it every time.

I think many of us miss God, miss the bigger picture, and lend ourselves to frustration when we try to figure out all the intricate details of how God is going to manifest a promise in our life. And even though God has already done everything for us that He is going to do, we sometimes get caught up in not knowing how a situation will turn out.

Trusting in the "not knowing" means even though you don't know specifically how the Lord will manifest His promises in your life, you still believe He will because He said it in His Word. The "not knowing" shouldn't be you not knowing *whether* the promise is going to come to pass. The "not knowing" should only be to the level of not knowing the specific details of *how* things are going to come to pass.

Had I known the avenue or path God would use to bless me with a new car, there would not have been a need for me to trust in a power higher than myself. I would have just sat around idly until the time came for me to go to the car dealership to take possession of my new car. The opportunities I had to use the Word of God to help me mature and grow as a person would not have been there.

As human beings, when there aren't things present that challenge us or apply pressure, there is often no personal growth. We *need to believe* in a greater power. I heard an anointed pastor say that we were never created to bear the weight of our own provision. We need God's help to make it in life. We also need each other to help encourage, support and be the extension of God's hand in this world.

As I was writing this, what came to mind was the storyline of a well-known movie called *Cast Away*.

In this movie, Tom Hanks' character, Chuck Noland, was the sole survivor in a plane crash that occurred over the Pacific Ocean during a storm. After somehow surviving the plane crash, he washed ashore onto a deserted island. From that moment, the plot takes you through the ups and downs, trials, and tribulations his character experienced while being alone with very limited resources on a deserted island.

For him, it quickly became about learning how to survive. While he had to learn how to survive physically (food, shelter, environmental factors beyond his control), the greater challenge would become how to survive mentally. The fear that undoubtedly plagued his heart and mind about never being found did eventually overwhelm him to the point of him contemplating and attempting suicide.

During this time, he felt the longing for companionship, so he created his friend Wilson out of a volleyball found in one of the packages that washed ashore right after the plane crash. Fast forward four years, a considerably thinner, rugged appearing Chuck Noland emerges...still somehow surviving.

One sunny day, he awoke to a noise. The noise was caused by a worn, broken piece of what appeared to be part of a discarded port-a-potty frame that washed ashore. The average person would have just considered this as scrap parts of junk metal that happened to make it a long journey to this island. But as Chuck sat and studied this piece of metal, survival mode began to kick in. He got an idea that would prove to be lifesaving.

He immediately began to come up with what turned out to be a well-thought-out and elaborate escape plan. He used what had washed ashore as a sail and built a raft made of wood from the island. He mapped out the best time he would need to execute his escape plan and how long he would have to finish building the raft before departure day. What one person would have likely considered as something insignificant ended up being the very thing that set him free.

For me, this entire story represents what many would describe as a truly hopeless situation, as everyone back in his hometown of Memphis, TN, had resolved to the belief that he had died in the plane crash. After 1500 days on a deserted island, he survived to tell his story despite all the odds.

The part of this story that stood out to me was when he was recounting his experience with his friend. He began discussing how he thought he was never going to get off that island. He was convinced he was going to die of sickness or an injury. The only thing he could control was how and when his death would occur. But when he went up to the summit to test his suicide plan, he recounts the weight of the log snapped the limb, so he couldn't even control his death.

After this event, he says a warm feeling came over him, and he knew, somehow, he had to stay alive. He had to keep breathing, even though there was no reason in the natural to hope. *Logic* and *reasoning* told him he would never see his home again. Then one day, all his logic was proven wrong after a tide came in and brought him a sail.

He had a picture of the love of his life, Kelly, with him while he was on the island. After his return, he learned she had moved on with her life and got married after they all thought he died in the crash. Before he left the island, he told his fictitious friend Wilson that he was scared. (Understand that when you're stepping out on faith, you must leave fear behind.) He really didn't know if he would have enough stamina to keep going a little longer, but he took a chance.

Despite all odds, he determined within himself to choose the "life" box instead of the "death" box. In that decision, he had to have faith that a ship of some sort would come along at just the precise moment to rescue him, so he wouldn't now die in the middle of the ocean after surviving on the island. Even though this is a fictitious story, I drew real-life applications from it.

The revelation I got from watching this movie was that while the island had become his new normal or a familiar place, he couldn't stay there. That familiar place would eventually be the place of his destruction if he didn't act. We may not always know the outcome, but there is always a reward in persevering and not giving up.

Even if you don't know the specific outcome of a situation, all you need to do is get a promise from God, and you can trust His voice. We don't have to know everything to trust our loving Father. Don't get distracted by wanting to know the entire plan before trusting that He has already made way for you.

The character Chuck Nolan said in the movie, even though he was sad to lose Kelly all over again, he was grateful she was with him during his darkest time. That image of her became like an anchor to his soul (getting an inner image of what you believe God for is a crucially important beginning step of faith). And now, in the new, unfamiliar place he found himself in, he knew what he had to do. He said he had to keep breathing because tomorrow the sun would rise, and who knew what the tide would bring in.

It may be a long, arduous journey to survival, but faith in God will not leave you shipwrecked and lost. Whatever your "island of impossibility" is, let your faith give substance to your hope, so everything you need and desire will be yours.

Is There Anything Too Hard for God?

You may find yourself asking this question: "Can I believe God for something like that?" Whatever your "that" is, the answer is yes! I sat in my office one day and thought about that question (and similar questions) we sometimes wonder and ponder over: questions and internal conflicts we may never verbalize.

There are just some situations we face in life that seem impossible. When you stop and think about the challenges you face, it honestly may seem as though there is no hope, but I find it too convenient to take the road that leads to hopelessness and defeat during dark despair.

In many hardships and challenges I've had to face in life, faith within me just will not allow me to cave in and quit during these times. We will all go through our share of valley experiences. The Bible says as much in the book of John 16:33 (NLT), "I have told you all this so that you may have peace in me. Here on earth, you will have many trials and sorrows. But take heart because I have overcome the world."

The fact that the sun rises every day gives me hope. Despite if it's a cloudy day, or a windy day or a snowy day, the sun still rises, and it's a new day, with new reasons to hope. One may not be able to appreciate the sun when it's cloudy outside, but the miracle is that even though you may not be able to see the rays...it's still there. The power of the sun's rays travels at a rate of about 186,000 miles per second. That is powerful! The sun has enough power to cause the darkness of night to cease, even though you may not be able to see it through a cloudy situation.

We live on a planet where we experience natural storms.

Some storms may be very momentary and fleeting, others may last a bit longer, but one thing is true, those storms never stay or last forever. So too, is true of the storms we face in life. They may come, but they never last forever. In some way, shape, or form, it will eventually come to an end. Since you know, they are only temporary, resist the temptation to quit in the middle of it. It may seem like you're going to cave in under the weight of it but use your hope and faith in God as an anchor.

What didn't work yesterday may work today. Give it more thought, look at it a different way or in a new light. Talk it through with someone else who may offer a different perspective that you did not think of. And sometimes it takes the passage of time for us to realize, you know what, maybe what I was going through wasn't that bad after all.

Everything seems bigger when you are standing in the middle of it. I encourage you to use your imagination, step out of your situation, and look at it from a bird's eye view. Look at it from the vantage point of heaven. When you take off in an airplane, the farther you get away from the structures and landscapes on the ground, the smaller and smaller those things begin to appear. Some people give up before they get to see the rainbow that comes after the rain.

In biblical history recorded in the book of Genesis, there is the story of a man named Noah. During Noah's time, there was a lot of wickedness in the earth. The imaginations and evil of man's heart had become so great, to the point where it grieved the Lord that He even made man, but the Bible described Noah as a "just man." He was righteous and blameless among the people of his time. So, God said to Noah He was going to end the violence in the earth by destroying mankind and the animals with a flood.

Noah was instructed to build an ark. God would cause it to rain forty days and forty nights, after which time the entire earth and everything in it would be destroyed. But because Noah was a righteous man, God established a covenant with him. God spared Noah, his entire house, as well as seven male and female pairs of each kind of animal and bird from being destroyed in the flood. After the flood was over, God made a promise to Noah that He would never again curse the ground nor destroy mankind with the waters of a flood.

And as a sign, or token, of this covenant, God created the rainbow in the clouds. Every time you see the rainbow, it is a remembrance of God's everlasting covenant between God and every living creature that is upon the earth. To this day, the rainbow remains a confirmation of that covenant. God said in Genesis 9:16 (NIV), "Whenever the rainbow appears in the clouds, I will see it and remember the everlasting covenant between God and all living creatures of every kind on the earth."

The Word of the Lord to you today is, don't give up…your harvest is coming! Don't give up before you reach your cruising altitude, where everything unimportant shrinks out of sight and ceases to be an issue as you soar into your destiny. Don't give up before you fulfill every desire of your heart. Don't give up and miss the glorious opportunity to see the sunshine that comes after the rain.

> *Life Application: Whenever you find yourself under pressure and think you can't make it another day, remember the words of Chuck Noland from Cast Away, and let it encourage your heart to stay in faith—Tomorrow the sun will rise; who knows what the tide will bring in.*

"Now thanks be unto God, which always causeth us to triumph in Christ..."

2 Corinthians 2:14 (KJV)

CHAPTER 8

FAITH THAT GETS RESULTS

Hope—A Necessary Component of Faith

In this chapter, I will discuss the process that led up to that Labor Day weekend event at a car dealership where I walked away with the keys to a debt-free brand-new car. As I begin this discussion, I want to talk more about hope and its importance when it comes to your faith.

As described in chapter 2, faith is the substance of things *hoped* for, the evidence of things not seen. Many people have hope, but not everyone has faith or confidence supporting their hope. The world operates on the premise of hope without any certainty of receiving. What I call "world hope," in contrast to "believer's hope," doesn't have the driving force of faith behind it. You hear phrases such as "I really do hope so" or "Yes, I'm hoping everything is okay." But many say this without any knowledge of the truth of faith's role in supporting their hope.

Hope for the believer is substantiated by faith, which we have learned comes by way of the Word of God. My faith in God is my proof that I will have what I say. I'm not just hoping for something that I'm not sure if it's really going to come to pass. The hope of a believer is not a blind hope or an empty hope. It's a hope that's assured it will happen because it already has in the spirit.

My complete surrender to God shows that I'm at rest and completely dependent upon Him for the manifestation. I'm not hoping in the position of not really being sure if I'm going to get it or not. A believer hopes to know with an established heart that I already have on the inside what I believed I received when I prayed. Thus, when it comes to having a winner's faith, hope is still a necessary component.

The word hope means to cherish a desire with anticipation; to want something to happen or to be true; to desire with expectation of obtainment or fulfillment. Since faith is the substance of things hoped for, you must first start with hope and don't throw away patience during the process. To eventually get to the end result of your desires, hope is a huge part of the process.

Romans 8:24–25 (NLT) states, "We were given this hope when we were saved. (If we already have something, we don't need to hope for it. But if we look forward to something we don't yet have, we must wait patiently and confidently.)" The Scripture also says in Ephesians 3:20 that God is able to do exceeding abundantly above all that we ask or think. Whatever you can dare to dream and ask God for, He can do even greater than that. This leads us to the importance of a healthy imagination, which is so important to your faith.

Looking once more at Proverbs 23:7, it says that you are as you think in your heart. We have already learned that the heart is the ground. The conception is taking place in your heart, which is being influenced by your thought life. Positive, healthy imagination is the blueprint that will begin to paint a picture of the promise on your heart and mind, moving you closer to manifestation.

Hope—An Anchor to the Soul

Referencing back to Abraham's life, the book of Hebrews reflects on God's promise made to him about becoming the father of many nations. It takes the Old Testament Scripture account of Abraham's life and depicts a very poignant summation of the power of God's covenant promise made to Abraham. It shows how Abraham's faith moved that promise from hope to reality. It's a lengthy passage, but I think it's worth reading with heartfelt intention because it reveals the devoted and unchanging heart of our loving Father. Hebrews 6:13-19 (NLT) reads,

> For example, there was God's promise to Abraham. Since there was no one greater to swear by, God took an oath in his own name, saying: "I will certainly bless you, and I will multiply your descendants beyond number." Then Abraham waited patiently, and he received what God had promised. Now when people take an oath, they call on someone greater than themselves to hold them to it. And without any

question that oath is binding. God also bound himself with an oath, so that those who received the promise could be perfectly sure that he would never change his mind. So, God has given both his promise and his oath. These two things are unchangeable because it is impossible for God to lie. Therefore, we who have fled to him for refuge can have great confidence as we hold to the hope that lies before us. This hope is a strong and trustworthy anchor for our souls. It leads us through the curtain into God's inner sanctuary.

Going back to the definition of faith, we can have great confidence in our hope because of faith (our reliance upon Christ). And just as grace establishes or settles our hearts to receive from God, hope is an anchor for the soul. Why? Because our hope is based upon something unchangeable—God's covenant promise. There is no divorcing out of this covenant. God cannot and would not go back on what He promised.

God's Word is everlasting, and it will never return void. If God spoke it, He will bring it to pass. This is the hope for the believer that begins with what we dare to think or imagine God to do for us. When we hope for something based on what God has spoken to us either personally or through His Word, we can begin to take the necessary steps to stand in faith for the manifestation of that promise, simply based on His unchangeable Word.

"Even when there was no reason for hope, Abraham kept hoping-believing that he would become the father of many nations...." (Romans 4:18, NLT). Even when there seems to be no reason to hope, start hoping and keep on hoping. Let faith in God do what others said would be impossible for you. This, dear reader, is how you tap into the faith that gets results.

From Faith to Manifestation

When I began to believe God for a new car debt-free, I didn't have a book or a manual guide entitled *The Ten-Step Guide on How to Get Guaranteed Results in Thirty Days or Less*. While I had a relationship with God at this time in my life, and I had believed God for other things prior to this, faith really was not something that I had a lot of experience with. I knew the Bible said we should walk by faith and live by faith, but I did not have a solid foundation of what it really meant to be a believer that totally relied on God for everything.

If you are a person that grew up in church and went to church because it's what you did on the weekends, you may have had this same "religious" experience that I had growing up. And if you did not grow up with a family that went to church, it's not something you should feel condemned about. There are many people who go to church and still don't have a true concept of the magnitude of how powerful faith really is for the believer.

Sometimes it's easier for a person who's never heard anything about faith to hear the pure gospel of Jesus Christ for the first time, receive it in their heart, and begin to move mountains in their life because of the power and revelation of the Word of God. I was raised in the church but never got to the place of developing a relationship with Jesus for myself. So, for many years, I did not value the Word to the point of reading it, believing it, and expecting it to become fruitful and flourish in my life.

During times where I should have had the faith of a winner, I had no power operating in my life because I had no Word. And thus, I was mentally agreeing with being a born-again Christian, but worry, doubt, and unbelief were still a strong undercurrent in many of the choices I made in my life. That "Pistis" faith, total reliance upon Christ for my salvation, was still not completely manifesting in my life.

The end of 2004 was the year that I bought my first home. This was two years after I graduated from college. With the Lord's help, I was able to qualify for a loan and went through the closing process relatively smoothly for a first-time homebuyer. At this point, I was still driving the car I had from college, which was a 1996 Nissan Sentra.

Approximately two years after buying my home, as my Nissan was getting older, the desire for a new car started to come up within me. Even though I was working full-time and living independently, I knew that a mortgage and a car note would be a bit of a stretch for me, given my income. My car was old, but it was in relatively good condition, so I didn't have the added pressure to buy or lease a new one.

Others would occasionally ask me when I was going to get a new car. I would shrug it off, but in my heart, I was thinking, "When the Lord blesses me with one." It wasn't until around 2007 that I heard a word of faith, which birthed a hope that I could not only get a new car, but I could get it for free. I would soon learn that the currency of faith would prove to be the evidence that I had a paid-for brand new car somewhere waiting for me to take possession of.

I. Heard Faith

"So then faith cometh by hearing, and hearing by the word of God" (Romans 10:17, KJV).

I was watching a television show on the Christian broadcast network entitled *The 700 Club* when I heard a man talking about believing God for a new motorcycle. While I don't recall the entire story's specifics, I can recount that he asked the Lord for a new motorcycle. But the part that stood out to me was that he was bold enough to ask the Lord if He would give it to him for free. Hearing his testimony of what God did for him by faith ignited and energized hope in me. If this man can believe God for a new motorcycle and God gave him one, I thought to myself, I can believe for a new car and not have to pay for it either.

II. Ask, Believe, Receive

"This is the reason I urge you to boldly believe for whatever you ask for in prayer-believe that you have received it and it will be yours" (Mark 11:24, TPT).

Hearing the word of faith about what God did for someone else is what became the seed that I received by faith for my new car. What I began to think was possible was conceived in my mind and then dropped down in my heart. I was familiar with this Scripture in Mark 11 that said whatever we desire, when we pray, if we believe we receive it, then we will have it. I recall standing on this Scripture in college when I was preparing to take my state boards for my nursing license. So that same day I heard the man's testimony on the television show, I asked God for my new car and asked if He could give it to me for free.

When you are standing in faith for something, I think it's important to be specific with God about what you want. In this case, I didn't have a preference of what type of car I wanted. My specifics were just that I wanted it new and debt-free. When you've been specific about what you believe for, you'll know when your harvest shows up, and you won't settle for anything less than what He's promised.

III. Imagination and Meditation

"I stay awake through the night, thinking about your promise" (Psalm 119:148, NLT).

As discussed in the earlier section, your imagination is part of what develops hope in you. Whatever you believe for, the key is to develop a picture, an inner image, of that promise in your mind. I took possession of a new car by faith before I ever tangibly received the keys to a new car. This is what I meant earlier in this book when I said you must have it before having it. In my heart, I began to see what I didn't see with my physical eyes. I would literally be riding down the road in my old Nissan, and when I saw a car that I liked, I would visualize myself driving that new car. I could imagine the new car's look, feel, and even the new car's smell. Meditating on the promise began to shape something tangible in me. And I maintained a level of expectancy, no matter if it seemed like nothing was happening.

> *Life Application: If you are standing in faith for a promise from God, meditate on His promises until that promise becomes more real to you than your current circumstances. Keep looking at what you are believing for until it makes an imprint on your heart.*

IV. Give Thanks

"And in the midst of everything be always giving thanks, for this is God's perfect plan for you in Christ Jesus" (1 Thessalonians 5:18, TPT).

As I continued to stand in faith for my new car, I continued on driving my old '96 Nissan, being grateful that I had a car to ride in. While it was getting older, I was grateful I had a car and did not have to rely on people or public transportation. I began to thank God for what I believed for, not knowing how it would happen or even when, for that matter. I remember thinking it didn't matter if God had someone buy me a new car or whether someone gave me the money for it; I just believed that somehow it was going to manifest.

I think it's important to note that I didn't constantly ask God for the same thing repeatedly. When I initially prayed and asked God for my new car, I believed I received it when I prayed. From that point forward, my position was from a place of thanksgiving and praise for what I believed God had already done. I believe that from the moment I prayed, God heard me. My faith turned a desire into a promise that went from the unseen to this physical world. When I would lay down at night, I say to the Father, "Thank you for my new car, and thank you for giving it to me for free." I don't even recall that I did this daily, but it never left my heart. Faith came by what I heard, and throughout this stance of faith, I clung to the hope that it was possible for me.

V. Harvest Time Has Come

Jesus also told them this parable: God's kingdom realm is like someone spreading seed on the ground. He goes to bed and gets up, day after day, and the seed sprouts and grows tall, though he knows not how. All by itself it sprouts, and the soil produces a crop; first the green stem, then the head on the stalk, and then the fully developed grain in the head. Then, when the grain is ripe, he immediately puts the sickle

166

to the grain, because the harvest time has come.

Mark 4:26-29 (TPT)

First, the Green Stem...

In the summer of 2008, I was at home when I heard a commercial announcement about a local car dealership that was having a summer car giveaway contest. I heard it and thought this sounds interesting. I didn't have many details about the contest, but I jotted down the information and decided that I would show up just to see what it was about. I went on the day of the event and got there toward the end when everything was pretty much over. I saw that a gentleman had just won a new electric car. As I walked around, getting more information about what had happened, one of the employees informed me this was one of two car giveaway contests that they had that summer. He went on to say that they were going to have another drawing in a few weeks to choose finalists for the next car giveaway. So, I went into the dealership and filled out my name on a couple of the entry tickets and placed them in the raffle box. It was free to enter, so I went for it.

Then the Head on the Stalk...

A few weeks later, I received a voicemail message on my answering machine stating I was a finalist in the car giveaway contest. When I heard that message, something inside of me leaped! This call really ignited my faith, and I had a knowing within me from that point forward that this was indeed the

167

Lord's hand, and something good was about to happen for me. After hearing the message that I knew this had to be God's harvest for me breaking through the ground, I was in so much anticipation. The promise I'd believed in was becoming ripe for harvest.

Then the Fully Developed Grain...

August 30th, 2008, was the day my harvest showed up in its full glory. After receiving the phone call about being a contestant finalist, I knew without any doubt that there would be no more need to hope for a new car after that day. My faith was about to connect me to supernatural manifestation. Going back to the Scripture in Hebrews 10:35-36 (TPT), it reads, "So don't lose your bold, courageous faith, for you are destined for a great reward! You need the strength of endurance to reveal the poetry of God's will and then you receive the promise in full."

For those that think God is a mystery and we can never know His will, I assure you, He wants to reveal His heart to those who will seek Him as Father. He is not a Father who withholds blessings from His children, and He's not the reason for all the calamity that happens in this world.

I encourage you to let those verses in Hebrews chapter 10 begin to plant the seed of faith in your heart about the reality of a loving God. God and His Word are One, so meditating on His promises will allow you to experience the reality of His goodness. If you desire to know God more, just ask Him to reveal His heart to you.

God loves when we are open and honest with Him from the sincerity of our hearts. If you ask Him, He will make Himself real to you. The reality of the risen Savior, Jesus Christ, will then cause you to develop a confidence that will become your reliance for every need in life. As a result, you will get to the place of knowing that faith in God will always yield a great reward.

Tailor-Made Promises

When you step out in faith to believe God for the abundant life that He promises you, He starts tailor-making His promises for you. We are all unique individuals, and God knows how to reach us where we are, but we have to be open to receive from Him.

The Scripture says a double-minded man is unstable in all of his ways, and those people should not think that they will receive anything from the Lord (James 1:7-8). Let your heart be single-minded where the things of God are concerned. If you find yourself struggling to receive from the Lord, don't be discouraged. If you're not there yet, you can get there! If you have lost hope because of the hardships you've experienced in life, I pray that you are re-energized to start dreaming again. Start to see your life as God says it can be.

The only way you can lose is if you never get started. Take a chance in life, and just step out, one small step at a time. I took a faith step and went down to the car lot just to see what was going on. I believed in God for a new car, so I figured it wouldn't hurt to go down to where a fleet of new cars was sitting around.

Faith is active! When you ask God for something according to His Word, He does His part. We must cooperate, listen for His voice to see if He's leading us to this place or that place, and just rest that He is tailoring—making your promise. And no matter what happens, don't quit in the middle of the process. Have patience because your faith is going to produce the manifestation.

God has good things in store for you, and He's already custom-designed your promises, just the way you like it. As you conclude this book, I'm standing in faith with you that every desire that you have will become a reality for you. As you have heard the Word of faith through my testimony, decide to step out on faith and believe God for what others have said is impossible.

"For when we place our faith in Christ Jesus, there is no benefit in being circumcised or being uncircumcised. What is important is faith expressing itself in love."

Galatians 5:6 (NLT)

CHAPTER 9

In Your Hope, Remember The Love

Love—The Expression of Faith

Here as we conclude the final chapter of your faith journey, we will look at one of the greatest forces that exist in this world—love. While we looked more at the "anatomy" of faith in chapter 2, we can liken this to the "physiology" of faith or how faith ultimately functions. According to the Word of God in Galatians 5:6, faith works by love. In the New Living Translation, it reads as "faith expressing itself in love." God, who is Love, never fails. If your faith is rooted in the love of God, it will never fail.

If you recall the account of Abraham's life, Abraham, along with every male in his house, underwent a *covenant* of circumcision as a sign of the covenant God made with him. This was God's confirming oath of the promise He made to Abraham of him being the father of many nations, as a result of a son being born to him and his wife. Here in the book of Galatians, we see the writer Paul giving the overall message to the Christians at Galatia that because of this new covenant that came by way of the sacrifice of Jesus, gentile believers do not have to submit to circumcision and the laws of Moses in order to be saved. Salvation is a free gift of grace and is totally dependent upon faith in Christ Jesus.

In Galatians 5:6 (KJV), it states, "...faith which worketh by love." The word "worketh" in the Greek means to be active, efficient; effectual (fervent).[17] To be fervent, or to have a zeal about something, means an ardent interest in the pursuit of something. And to be efficient means "capable of producing desired results with little or no waste (as of time or materials).[18]" Because of God, who is love, standing in faith will produce the desired results, and it is never a waste of time. Even if you come to realize you missed it along the way but thought you were in faith, there is something to be gained from that. Every mishap in life, God can turn around and use it for His glory.

Going back to the discussion on the established heart, it can also be deduced that establishing your heart with grace means having the spiritual insight and conviction of what the finished work of Christ Jesus has done for you, influence your heart to the point that it permanently settles you. Love (God) sent Jesus to the Cross of Calvary to die for us. When the magnitude of what love did for us while we were sinners pierces you to the point of complete conviction, that love is expressed in the form of faith. When you know and believe the love God has for you, faith will be an automatic byproduct of that love.

17   James Strong, 1995
18   Merriam-Webster, 2019

While you start first with hope and allow faith to be your confidence, don't forget the love. Don't forget that God loves you so much. He sent His Son to die for you. The only reason God did that was to have you back. He lost His covenant relationship with mankind in the Garden of Eden. The only way He could get you back was, over time, allowing Jesus to be born by way of fallen people so that He (as a righteous man) could legally redeem fallen mankind back to their position as sons and daughters of God.

Romans 8:32 (TPT) says, "For God has proved his love by giving us his greatest treasure, the gift of his Son. And since God freely offered him up as the sacrifice for us all, he certainly won't withhold from us anything else he has to give." What need do you have today? If God freely gave us His Son, do you not think that He would freely give you everything else you need in life?

God is not withholding any good thing from us. Why would He send Jesus to die for your salvation (prosperity, healing, deliverance) and then turn around and withhold these blessings from you? That would be a waste of a sacrifice and wouldn't make sense to any rational person. God is love, and your faith in Him should be born out of the knowledge of His love for you.

Love Heals, Love Forgives

Hebrews 12:1 tells us we must take off the heavyweights of life and the sin which tries to keep us in bondage. The next verse says we need to be attentive to Jesus, who is the Author and Finisher of our Faith. It presents what I think is a beautiful picture of love in action:

> We look away from the natural realm and we fasten our gaze onto Jesus who birthed faith within us and who leads us forward into faith's perfection. His example is this: Because his heart was focused on the joy of knowing that you would be his, he endured the agony of the cross and conquered its humiliation, and now sits exalted at the right hand of the throne of God!
>
> Hebrews 12:2 (TPT)

In Christ Jesus, you and I are worthy to receive God's love, healing, power, and forgiveness. You must put aside sin because it brings with it a spirit of death, it damages your soul, and it gives you a guilty conscience. Your faith in God will not work with a guilty conscience.

When Adam and Eve disobeyed and sinned against God, the first thing they did was hide. They lost the light of God, their spiritual eyes were opened, and they began to know each other by the flesh versus by the spirit. They now knew good and evil, and they were afraid. So instead of being full of love, they were now full of fear. That's what sin does. It gets you to focus on yourself and what you've done instead of focusing on Jesus and what He's done.

But thank God for Jesus! He knew as a result of Adam's disobedience; we were all made sinners. But because of the obedience of Jesus, we would all have a chance to now be restored back to righteousness. This is a reflection and revelation of the great love God has for us. We can look at Jesus' life and His walk of faith and pattern our life after Him. He was faithful all the way to the cross. Once we are born-again, that seed of faith moves on the inside of us. If Jesus was faithful, I can now be faithful. I can take the Word of God, sow it in my heart, and watch it bring life, just as Jesus brought us all life.

From the foundation of the world, faith made the world, framed humanity from dust, and set a course through time to redeem lost mankind back to God. And it continues to work in us today through the resurrected Savior living in us. If you are trying to receive from God but are still carrying around a guilty, sin-stained conscience, Jesus' Blood is the only way for you to be free of this.

Hebrews 9:14 (NIV) says, "How much more, then, will the blood of Christ, who through the eternal Spirit offered himself unblemished to God, cleanse our consciences from acts that lead to death, so that we may serve the living God." Like everything else in the kingdom of God, you must receive a cleansed, guilt-free conscience by faith. We are saved by faith, we believe that we are forgiven by faith, we believe that we are new creations by faith, and we must know that God does not hold our past against us once we give Him our life.

God can do something with the sin; He can handle your

177

mistakes. The only thing He can't do something with is you're not believing in His power of love that forgives and heals you. The Bible says in Hebrews 8:12 that God does not remember our sins and iniquities anymore once we accept Jesus as our Lord. Jesus has made us whole. We must let go of every dead weight that will keep us from freely receiving our wholeness.

You were not created to carry the weight of sin or the results of sin on your back. If you were to imagine how that looks in the spirit realm, imagine a person hunched over and barely able to walk due to a massive amount of weight on their back. This is not the picture of a person who has faith in God. This is a picture of someone who is walking around in self-effort, carrying a weight that only God is equipped to carry. Instead of casting all their care on God, they are carrying it themselves.

Sin, and the weight of it, was too much for mankind to handle. If we could have handled sin, God would have left Adam and Eve alone and told them to figure it out. Faith is a life that is totally yielded and totally surrendered to God. God wants all of you—spirit, soul, and body. During what could be a loud and chaotic daily life experience, God wants your mind so that He can keep you in perfect peace no matter the circumstances that may be going on around you.

Being totally surrendered is turning every issue, every problem, and every concern over unto the Lord to the point where it's no longer a part of your thought life. In your heart, you believe God loves you; therefore, you have nothing to fear. Totally surrendered means you're not walking around

178

with symptoms of "dis-ease" inwardly because of worry and anxiety over life's issues. You can go to sleep at night and truly be at peace because you know God will not mismanage your life.

Total reliance upon Christ means you learn how to rest in God. Resting means you are abiding in a place in God where you are free from labor and having peace of mind continually. By faith, it is possible to live this kind of life. In Hebrews 4:1, the Scripture tells us we must endeavor and be diligent about entering into the rest of God. This is the good fight of faith.

By faith, learn how to relax and let God handle the weights of your life. Let the Blood of Jesus flow over all the scars that came upon your heart from the corruption of this world and receive that supernatural healing and restoration that can only come from Him.

Find Your Freedom

If you find yourself with a heavy heart because of regrets or mistakes of the past, realize that it is very hard to go forward if you keep looking in the rearview mirror. This is what the Lord spoke to me concerning finding freedom: "You keep being consumed by your past—the mistakes you've made, the things that have happened to you. Everyone goes through challenges in this life. No one is exempt. Don't be overcome by the challenges in life. Use what has happened to you to make you better, stronger, wiser, and to be a blessing to someone else by sharing how you overcame. Get over it, so you can help someone else."

I encourage you to do the same. Let go of the guilt, shame of things you might have done, or anything that may be hindering you from receiving from God. God's love for us doesn't take account of any suffered wrongs. It is in Him that we find our freedom.

So it doesn't matter what mistakes we've made in the past. Don't allow the guilt and condemnation that tries to come, make you think you're not worthy of a promise or that you're not worthy for the blessing of God to be on your life. If something does not happen in your life and you are dealing with guilt, shame, and condemnation, it is preventing you from going forward in Christ as a free man or woman. It's an issue of the heart that will ultimately affect your harvest.

Guilt and shame are blessing blockers. Let it go. You are worthy to receive everything God has for you. Don't go another day, allowing these negative emotions to hinder what God wants to do in your life. Don't let these things stifle your faith and cause the Word to be unfruitful. Allow God's love to heal you from the inside out. Let Him restore your soul and make you completely whole. This places you in the right position to obtain your promise.

In the book of Psalms, God said, "As far as the east is from the west, so far hath he removed our transgressions from us" (Psalm 103:12, KJV). If sin (our past mistakes, sin nature, consequences of sin) was placed on Jesus, done away with, and buried at the cross, then it no longer belongs to us as believers in Christ. Once you give it to Jesus, forget about it because it's no longer yours. You must give every concern and every care to Jesus and allow His Blood that was shed on Calvary to purge your conscience of it. In the records of heaven, we are completely whole in Jesus. Everything we need is already done.

No Fear in Love

Faith expresses itself in love, not fear. If you are in fear, you are halting the opportunity for faith to be operative in your life. Since the Bible talks about fear having torment, it would be safe to conclude that if you are fearful in an area where you want to receive from God, you are inflicting unnecessary punishment on yourself and halting God's ability to move in your life. This is what John wrote to Christians about this topic:

We have come into an intimate experience with God's love, and we trust in the love he has for us. God is love! Those who are living in love are living in God, and God lives through them. By living in God, love has been brought to its full expression in us so that we may fearlessly face the day of judgment, because all that Jesus now is, so are we in this world. Love never brings fear, for fear is always related to punishment. But love's perfection drives the fear of punishment far from our hearts. Whoever walks constantly afraid of punishment has not reached love's perfection. Our

181

love for others is our grateful response to the love God first demonstrated to us.

1 John 4:16-19 (TPT)

One of the most important points I hope you really take with you as you go about walking out your life of faith is that God's love for you is everlasting and unchanging. If God is in you, there should not be fear dwelling in you. There is no fear in God, which means there is no fear in His Word. You can believe the Word without fear of it not coming to pass. But remember, God's blessings over our lives are not automatic. We must get Wisdom for life from the Word of God, know what we, as believers of Christ Jesus, have rights to, and enforce our authority for what is rightfully ours on this earth.

We must contend for the faith and stand in what seems like impossible situations and declare what God said over it. When your hope seems to want to fade with time, still your soul and think about what love has done for you. God so loved the world that He gave His very best for you. Remember the sacrifice Jesus made for you, and rest in the knowledge of that love. "...what you hope for is kept safe for you in heaven. You first heard about this hope when you believed the true message, which is the good news" (Colossians 1:5, CEV).

Don't ever lose hope in those dreams that you have for your life. God is keeping it safe for you in heaven. But it will require your faith to make it a reality in your life.

> *Life Application: "Until then, there are three things that remain: faith, hope, and love—yet love surpasses them all. So above all else, let love be the beautiful prize for which you run" (1 Corinthians 13:13, TPT). The greatest gift that we have been given in this world is the love of a Father to his beloved children. Faith in that love guarantees you the victory!*

Be Made Whole

First Thessalonians 5:23-24 (NIV) says, "May God himself, the God of peace, sanctify you through and through. May your whole spirit, soul and body be kept blameless at the coming of our Lord Jesus Christ. The one who calls you is faithful, and he will do it." This is my prayer over you today. No matter where you are in your life, I pray that the supernatural power of God's love makes you whole—spirit, soul, and body.

I hope you have been empowered by the words that have been imparted into your heart by reading *A Winner's Faith*. I also hope you have enjoyed taking this faith journey as much as I have enjoyed writing it through the inspiration of the Holy Spirit.

You are worthy of receiving everything that your heart desires because God has given you those desires. He loves you and wants you to have a joyous and prosperous life. Trust Him today. Give Him your full heart today. Don't compromise the Word today. Establish your heart in Grace today. God will always respond to faith. If God said it, you can believe in it.

Make a quality decision to choose the "life" box today and continue to walk in the way of abundant life. Don't let Satan, the enemy of faith, rob you of another day of what rightfully belongs to you as a kingdom citizen. I pray God's very best for you as you go forward, conquering and winning in this life!

If you are dealing with circumstances that appear hopeless, empty, or lifeless, I urge you to act on what you've heard through reading this book. I encourage you to give voice to the concluding words of this faith journey's final poetic epilogue. Read it aloud so that it is heard by your own ears, seen by your own eyes, and is planted in your own heart. As you begin to speak these words in faith, you are actively speaking life back into the situation.

Remember that everything you need in life has already been finished through the sacrifice of Jesus. What you speak by faith will come into agreement with what God has already done in the spirit realm. You and the Word will become one. This is where the power lies. As you read it, believe it with all your heart, and continue to confess these words until you begin to see a change. It is written in the first person as if you are speaking it over yourself, but you can change the tense if you are standing in faith for someone else.

With *Your* heart, you believe, and with *Your* mouth, *Your* confession will be made to be *Your* salvation. Let go of all fear, stand still, and you will see and experience the deliverance, victory, prosperity, and saving power of the Lord. Faith in your heart, coupled with speaking forth God's Word with thanksgiving and praise, will begin to cause healing, wholeness, and restoration in every area of your life.

Amid life's challenges, remember the words of Jesus to His disciples, "Have faith in God." Irrespective of what's going on in the natural, faith in God alone secures the victory and makes you a winner.

BODY - THE EPILOGUE

THE DAY LOVE HEALED ME

Lord, all that You have done
Let it remain in me,
Spirit…Soul…. Body.
Lord, manifest Your Glory in me,
Manifest healing in me.
There is no fear in this Love
Perfect Love has expelled fear out of me
What You have done, reveal it to me.
Show me how powerful the Word can be,
When I believe, rely on and trust in thee.
Lord, manifest strength in me
So that even others may clearly see
How Grace upon Grace has set me free.
Herein I boldly declare Your truth over me ~
Yes, my Lord has saved me (Spirit).
Yes, my Lord has restored me (Soul).
Yes, my Lord has healed me (Body).

In the middle of trouble
I say, "Light in me…BE!"
Be the change inside of me!
Wash me, mold me, purify me
Be the Wholeness personified in me…
For this is the day, Love has healed me.

———

BIBLIOGRAPHY

1. Amplified Bible (AMP), Lockman Foundation

2. "Dictionary.com LLC" https://www.dictionary.com/

3. Martini, Frederic H., PhD. *Fundamentals of Anatomy and Physiology,* 4th Edition. Prentice Hall, Inc., 1998.

4. Hinn, Benny "The Gifts of the Holy Spirit, Part 2." Benny Hinn Ministries–Home/E-Newsletter. 2019. https://www.bennyhinn.org/enewsletter/gifts-of-the-holy-spirit-part-2/

5. Strong, James. LL.D., S.T.D. *The New Strong's Exhaustive Concordance of the Bible.* Thomas Nelson Publishers, 1995.

6. "Merriam-Webster, Incorporated" https://www.merriam-webster.com/

7. New Living Translation (NLT)

8. The Holy Bible, King James Version (KJV). Cambridge Edition: 1769.

9. The Message (MSG), Eugene Peterson, NavPress

10. The New International Version (NIV)

11. The Passion Translation (TPT)–Passion and Fire Ministries

12. "Why-It-Matters. Language Nutrition." Talk With Me Baby–Why Talking Matters. 2019. http://www.talkwithmebaby.org/language_nutrition

ABOUT THE AUTHOR

Early in life, Takieya J. Jones never thought about the possibility of becoming a published author after years of suppressing a passion for writing that was buried by a spirit of fear. She has always wanted to help others, which led her down an early career path in the healthcare field, where she has spent the last eighteen years working in the pediatric acute and community care settings. Takieya is now pursuing a God-given calling to be an instrument of healing to people's physical and spiritual needs. She is currently obtaining an associate degree in biblical studies and desires to minister hope and ignite a passion for Jesus to people worldwide through her writing and other ministry gifts. She is a Holy-Spirit-filled believer who wants a dying and lost world to know that Jesus is alive, and there is nothing impossible for those who believe.